Colorado Homes

Colorado Homes

By SANDRA DALLAS

With Photographs by
Kendal Atchison and Sandra Dallas

University of Oklahoma Press : Norman and London

OTHER BOOKS BY SANDRA DALLAS

Gaslights & Gingerbread (Denver, 1965; reprint, Athens, Ohio, 1984)
No More Than Five in a Bed (Norman, 1967)
Cherry Creek Gothic (Norman, 1971)
Sacred Paint (Kansas City, 1979)
Colorado Ghost Towns and Mining Camps (Norman, 1984)

Library of Congress Cataloging-in-Publication Data

Dallas, Sandra.
   Colorado homes.

   Bibliography: p. 247.
   Includes index.
   1. Dwellings—Colorado—Pictorial works.   2. Architecture, Domestic—Colorado—Pictorial works.   3. Colorado—Description and travel—
1981–   —Views.   I. Atchison, Kendal.   II. Title.
F777.D28   1986   978.8   86–40070
ISBN 0–8061–2004–5 (alk. paper)

The paper in this book meets the guidelines for permanence and durability of
the Committee on Production Guidelines for Book Longevity of the Council
on Library Resources, Inc.

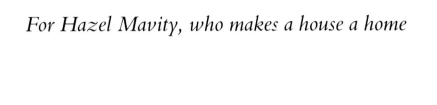

For Hazel Mavity, who makes a house a home

Contents

Acknowledgments

I DON'T KNOW THE NAMES of a great many of the people who helped with this book. They include the men in Sugar City who stopped working on a car one morning to talk with me about the houses the National Sugar Manufacturing Company built for its executives. In Rico there was a couple who waved me into their house one cold spring evening to tell me its fascinating history. The list also includes the service station attendants, the chambers of commerce secretaries, the owners of antique shops, the waitresses, and the historic house volunteers who cheerfully told me about their towns and architecture, or who gave me directions when I asked: "Where's the best old house in town?" It didn't seem appropriate to whip out a notebook and demand their names.

A great many people who helped me are not anonymous, however. As always, I am grateful to the staff of the Western History Department of the Denver Public Library, particularly to Augie Mastrogiuseppe, and to the Colorado Historical Society and Jim Teliha. Preservationists Beth Downs in Denver and Jim Munch in Pueblo were invaluable guides to their cities. Betty Smith, Lottie Reddert, Sally Plummer, Janet O'Connell, Nell Brown Propst, Jill and Ted Lee, Anne McLaughlin Long, and Ron Crutchfield, as well as Lockett Ford Ballard, Jr., and James R. DeMersman at Rosemount, Helen Katz at the Georgetown Society, and Marne Jurgemeyer in Fort Collins went out of their way to tell me the histories of some of the more interesting houses. B & W Photo Lab supplied both good work and good advice. Architect Paul Atchison was a wonderful source of information on the domestic architecture of the 1930s.

Once again, Ed Shaw, who suggested this project, Joaquin Rogers, and John Drayton, all of the University of Oklahoma Press, have made this book a pleasant experience.

I am grateful once more to my uncomplaining travel companion, Bob Atchison, and to my daughter and photographer, Kendal Atchison, who set us off on this project. The first book we did together, *Colorado Ghost Towns and Mining Camps,* was fun. This one has been sheer joy.

Sandra Dallas

Colorado Homes

Introduction

COLORADO WAS SETTLED BY PEOPLE who did not plan to stay. They were fortune hunters—gold and silver seekers—who expected to strike it rich within weeks or, better yet, days and then return home, set for life.

At first they gave no thought to building homes. A fortified

Mesa Verde. The first permanent homes in Colorado were cliff dwellings. *Author's Collection.*

3

Site unknown. For generations, nomadic Plains Indians lived in tipis made from buffalo hides. Tipis could be quickly erected or disassembled. *Courtesy Denver Public Library Western History Department.*

tent, a log cabin, or a dugout would see them through the winter. No need for a fancy house.

But after the first few months, they talked less of going back. Gold and silver eluded most of them, but they found something else, a good place to live. They discovered that even though a man might not make a fortune in Colorado, he could earn a decent living for himself and his family—at least a better one than he could back home. The fortune hunters became settlers.

The men talked of cities; the women talked of homes. The men settled the West; the women domesticated it. The women insisted that the log cabins with their mud floors and peeling walls be replaced with respectable houses. For the women, houses meant civilization.

In building homes, Coloradans were not initiators but imitators. Rather than develop original styles of architecture, they utilized architectural designs developed for other parts of the United States and even Europe, adapting them to Colorado's ter-

rain and climate. A Colorado Italianate house would have looked
at home in Galena, Illinois; a shingle-style house would have been
familiar to Newport, Rhode Island; and a mansard would have
blended in anywhere in the country. Even what might be called
"native" architecture was imported. The adobes came from New
Mexico, the soddies from Nebraska.

Homesick for wherever they had come from, the settlers often
transplanted their favorite styles of domestic architecture to Colorado, no matter how inappropriate to the western climate. There
was a hodge-podge of architecture in the state. Not long after the
turn of the century, Colorado visitor Julian Street, a travel writer
from the East, described Colorado Springs, which was wealthier
but not altogether unlike other booming Colorado towns:

> Homes are of every variety of architecture, and are inhabited by
> a corresponding variety of people. You will see half-timbered
> English houses, built by Englishmen and Scots; Southern colo-
> nial houses built by people from the South Atlantic States; New
> England Colonial houses built by families who have migrated
> from the regions of Boston and New York; one-story houses
> built by people from Hawaii, and a large assortment of the

San Juan Mountains. Gold seekers built rough
shelters on precarious sites high above timberline
to protect themselves during summer prospecting.
But in winter, the shacks were boarded up and left
to the winds. *Author's Collection.*

5

houses ranging from Queen Anne to Cape Cod cottages, and from Italian villas to Spanish palaces. There is even the Grand Trianon . . . and an amazing Tudor castle. . . .

To make things even more confusing, Coloradans mixed styles with abandon, making classification by architectural type today arbitrary and sometimes impossible.

The first native dwellings, of course, were whatever could be made from the earth. Colorado Indians built cavelike dwellings of mud and sticks and faced them south, like today's solar homes, to catch the rays of the sun. These early houses were so well constructed that they have stood for a thousand years in southwestern Colorado.

Long after the cave dwellers migrated south, nomadic Indians roamed Colorado, taking their dwellings with them—tipis made of animal skins stretched on lodgepoles that could be erected or disassembled quickly. Buffalo robes spread on the ground and tipi linings hung from the walls made them warm and relatively draft-free.

Site unknown. With the first cries of "gold!" prospectors rushed to remote mountain locations and put up tents to provide shelter from rain and snow. Within a few days hundreds of men resided in these temporary tent cities. *Courtesy Denver Public Library Western History Department.*

Poughkeepsie Gulch. With a stream nearby for washing clothes, an iron stove for cooking, and sturdy wooden chairs packed in on burros, summer living in a tent was pleasant. In winter, however, howling blizzards dumped heavy snow on this campsite at Red Mountain Pass. *Courtesy Denver Public Library Western History Department.*

Early white settlers brought their houses with them in the form of covered wagons and canvas tents. For example, Augusta Tabor, whose husband, Horace Austin Warner Tabor, was to become Colorado's premier silver king, arrived in 1859 with a seven-by-nine-foot tent she made herself. As soon as the Tabor wagon pulled into Idaho Springs, the tent was erected on a log foundation, and Horace Tabor went prospecting.

As Colorado rushed pell-mell toward respectability, its towns underwent a building boom that left visitors agog with the diversity and pretentiousness of its houses. Log cabins fell to gingerbread cottages that in turn gave way to stone castles. After the turn of the century, homes became simpler as the rich replaced ostentation with elegance, and the middle class became urban homeowners. During the 1920s and 1930s, Colorado had a brief fling with the international and art moderne styles.

To some extent, Colorado's domestic architecture was divided

7

Salida. Once civilization set in, tent living was acceptable only for campers. Whether the residents of this tent, with their iron bed and bicycle, are vacationers or squatters is unknown. *Courtesy Denver Public Library Western History Department.*

into three geographic zones: mountain, plains, and Front Range. The strike-it-rich miners who settled the mountain towns produced a decorative carpenter Gothic style, while their more restrained counterparts on the eastern plains stuck to unadorned frame cottages. The economically and socially diverse settlers along the Front Range embraced not only carpenter Gothic and eastern plains Spartan but every other style that was produced in America or in Europe.

Many Colorado towns had one predominant style that was determined by the caprices of a single builder or was the specialty of a local craftsman. The most distinctive houses in Silver Plume, for example, have large windows with rounded tops that are outlined with small squares of stained glass. Houses in Victor and Cripple Creek feature second-story bay windows that hang over the street. Salida is dotted with tiny mansards, while Central City sports board-and-batten construction. In towns along the Clear Creek—Idaho Springs, Dumont, and Georgetown—houses have wooden quoins. Kiowa has shingle-covered bungalows; Burlington has clipped gable roofs. Many of the houses around Kim are built of stone.

Even the larger cities, while boasting more architectural diversity, had pronounced preferences. Shingle-style mansions were more popular in Colorado Springs than anywhere else in the state, and there were so many stolid "four square" brick houses built in Denver that they were dubbed "Denver squares."

In large part, Colorado's homes themselves dictated the organization and direction of *Colorado Homes*. What began as a book about some of the state's most notable houses has evolved into a study of the richness and diversity of domestic architecture in Colorado.

Divide. Colorado homebuilders were ingenious. From the earliest times they turned any available material into shelter. *Kendal Atchison*

1. Log Cabins

You have no idea how nice Will and I are fixed up. . . . We have a nice door with an old-fashioned wooden latch, with the string on the outside, of course. The fireplace . . . is made of sods. In the southeast corner is the bunk; in the northwest corner the window, four panes of glass with sash. On the north side, between the end of the bed and the fireplace, we have two shelves and a bench. . . . We cut the meat on the bench and set water buckets on the other two shelves. . . . You have no idea how comfortable we all live. We sleep warm and nice.

THE LETTER, written in late 1858 by Denver founder William Larimer, Jr. to reassure his family that he and his son Will were safe from the frontier's hardships, describes one of the first cabins built in Denver at what is now the corner of Fifteenth and Larimer streets. General Larimer was not exaggerating. After the drafty tents and wagons that had been their home crossing the plains, the little log cabin, fitted with panes of glass—a luxury on the plains—was indeed "warm and nice," so snug, in fact, that the two men could shun the warmth of saloons and gambling dens and spend their evenings reading the Bible and *David Copperfield* by candlelight.

The first permanent dwellings in Denver and in the towns that sprang up in the mountains to the west were log cabins. They could be built from materials the pioneers found on hand and were easy and quick to erect. The size of a cabin was dictated by the height of the pine trees used to construct it, and most were squares with walls about twelve feet long, made of logs that were notched at each end. If the builder was a perfectionist, and few were, he used his ax to square the logs, making them fit tighter and giving the dwelling a more finished appearance.

Rarely were glass or nails used in those first log cabins. Cracks were chinked with mud, though author Gene Fowler recalled that his grandfather's cabin near Empire was chinked with a tantalizing mixture of lime, creek sand, and aged burro manure.

Roofs were constructed of logs covered with twigs, dirt, and

Denver. Scores of log cabins like this one, which the *Rocky Mountain Herald* claimed was the first house built in Denver, were thrown up at the confluence of the South Platte River and Cherry Creek after the first gold seekers arrived in 1858. *Courtesy Denver Public Library Western History Department.*

Blanca Peak vicinity. Built with native materials and chinked with mud, log cabins were the first permanent dwellings to go up in the mountain mining camps. If the camp lasted more than a few weeks, homeowners added such amenities as glass windows. Peaked roofs would stand up to heavy snows better than flat ones. The outside table and the dishpan hung on the wall suggest that in the summer months household work took place outdoors. *Courtesy Denver Public Library Western History Department.*

sod. They kept out the worst of the snow and rain but were far from weatherproof. Following a storm, an unhappy homeowner noted: "The rains usually continued indoors for three or four days after they had ceased outside." Twin sisters who lived with their husbands in a double log cabin in Boulder covered everything in their house with rubber horse blankets when it rained, to keep the mud roof from oozing onto the furnishings.

Sometimes a corner fireplace made of mud or sod with a mud-plastered stick chimney provided heat as well as a cooking fire, but the affluent installed cook stoves, which were both safer and easier to use. Furnishings were sparse; there might be chairs and a bedstead made from branches that had been hacked off the logs that were used for walls; boxes would be used for bureaus or cupboards; and perhaps there would be a piece or two of precious furniture the settlers had hauled overland.

Augusta Tabor recalled arriving in California Gulch (later Lead-

Willow Creek. This family used its log house well into the twentieth century. The structure was inexpensive to build and easy to maintain, requiring only chinking each spring and fresh branches to hold down the sod roof. *Courtesy Colorado Historical Society.*

East of **Eagle.** Log cabins proved durable even if their residents did not. The remains of many such dwellings can be found in the Colorado mountains. This cabin has a sod roof. *Kendal Atchison*

13

Fraser. Though the size of a log cabin was limited by the height of the trees used to build it, the cabin could be enlarged by adding rooms. Some cabins took on the ungainly demeanor of a train. *Kendal Atchison*

Site unknown. Inside, a miner's cabin could be almost homey. These friends have probably shared a bountiful dinner of meat and potatoes served from the homemade table. There is a jug of local brew and even a violin, carefully hung on a nail on the wall, to provide entertainment. *Courtesy Colorado Historical Society*.

14

ville) and moving into a cabin built of green logs "without floor, door or window." The wagon in which she arrived was turned into a table, a sideboard, and some three-legged stools, and with nothing more to work on, she began taking in boarders, feeding them tough beef and dried apple pie.

Some prospectors attached hinged bunks to the walls of their cabins and fastened them up during the day in order to have more floor space. Legend has it that the bunks so intrigued drummer George Pullman that he copied them as sleeping berths in railroad cars.

Mementos of home were a treasured part of the decor. "If the numerous young women of New York and Boston could know that their photographs were the only bright spots in a log-cabin . . . they would be moved with great content," Richard Harding Davis noted after visiting cabins in Creede in 1892.

The more fastidious cabin dwellers sewed together flour or coffee sacks for carpets and decorated the walls with newspapers, placed right side up so they could be read at leisure. The custom

Goldfield. Before the owners deserted this cabin, they updated it with tall, stylish Victorian windows. *Kendal Atchison*

Leadville. Mining magnate James V. Dexter built a series of houses and hunting boxes throughout Colorado. On the outside, Dexter Cabin, built at the height of the Leadville silver boom, was a typical small log cabin. (Now a museum) *Kendal Atchison*

Inside, Dexter Cabin was a tribute to its builder, a connoisseur who collected Chinese ivory, jade, jewels, and oil paintings and ordered his social invitations from Tiffany's. The cabin resembled Dexter's lavish Denver home with walnut and maple floors, lace curtains, carved furniture, and elegant light fixtures. *Courtesy Colorado Historical Society.*

of papering log cabin walls with newspapers persisted well into the twentieth century, when miners were partial to the florid pink pages of the *Denver Post*.

One Denver lady covered her log walls with tablecloths and sheets, while a reporter for *Scribner's Monthly* noted after an 1879 visit to Leadville that artist-author Mary Hallock Foote and her mining engineer husband papered their cabin with building paper.

Breckenridge. Hand-hewn logs gave a better appearance and tighter fit to a cabin. Hewn logs used in the gable and a wood-encased stovepipe meant this cabin was built to last. (Now a museum) *Kendal Atchison*

One side was used as a wainscoting, and the other side, which was oak-grained, was placed above as a wallpaper. Pine strips, painted black, hid the seams. Mrs. Foote stretched the building paper between the roof beams to form a ceiling and hung United States Geological Survey maps on the walls as pictures.

In her "cabin by the ditch," as Mrs. Foote called it, she entertained visiting dignitaries with all the aplomb of a gentlewoman at home in the East. One guest was Helen Hunt Jackson, author of *Ramona,* who warned her hostess that it was unnatural to live in a place where "grass would not grow . . . and cats could not live." Other guests were enchanted. Rossiter Raymond, a noted mining man who was the Footes' guest, later wrote a rapturous poem about the little house:

> Let princes live and sneeze in their place of ease,
> Let colds and influenzas plague the rich,
> But give to me instead, a well ventilated head
> In a little log cabin on the Ditch!

17

Dumont. This nineteenth-century relic shows the durability of hewn-log construction. Two structures were combined to form a large cabin that may have served as a commercial structure. *Kendal Atchison*

Manassa. William Harrison Dempsey, the ninth of Hiram Dempsey's eleven children, was born in the Mormon community of Manassa. After young Dempsey changed his name to Jack and became known worldwide as the "Manassa Mauler," the family's one-room cabin was turned into a tourist attraction. (Now a museum) *Sandra Dallas*

Sunshine. A hewn-log miner's cabin has been modernized with electricity and a television antenna. *Sandra Atchison*

Denver. Although the chinking has fallen out, the window is broken, and the foundation is crumbling, this cabin, probably built in the 1860s, was still a snug residence at the turn of the century. *Courtesy Colorado Historical Society.*

19

Breckenridge. Naturalist Edwin Carter killed and mounted hundreds of animals and displayed them in his home. Carter's collection was acquired by the Denver Museum of Natural History. *Kendal Atchison*

East of **Eagle.** What began as a plain, square log cabin was later adorned with a shed-roof porch supported by turned columns, a frame addition, and a fine bay window. The house is abandoned, nonetheless. *Kendal Atchison*

Ouray. In 1882, Abbie and Charles Wheeler purchased a log cabin and turned it into this handsome house. When Wheeler died, his widow married his nephew. The house was kept in the family until 1929. *Sandra Dallas*

For more than forty years, through scores of gold and silver strikes, log cabins were the first houses built in Colorado mining camps. Unlike other kinds of first-generation architecture, such as sod houses and dugouts, log cabins lasted for years with no maintenance, and remnants of hundred-year-old log cabins can be seen in scores of Colorado ghost towns.

Moreover, log cabins were not necessarily abandoned for frame houses when the owners grew prosperous. Many cabins gained second stories or additional rooms built of frame. The mud chinking was replaced with cement, doors and windows were cut into the logs, and gingerbread trim was nailed to the roof. Sometimes entire cabins were covered with siding.

Many remained just as they were, however, and in later years log cabins developed a kind of rustic cachet. City dwellers built log cabins, some of them the size of small villas, as mountain retreats. Even today, many mountain dwellers prefer log construction to masonry or frame. Some 125 years later, Colorado residents, like the Larimers, in earlier times, sleep "warm and nice" in log cabins.

The Wheeler house in Ouray's heyday. *Courtesy Denver Public Library Western History Department.*

21

2. Adobes and Soddies

ON THE EASTERN PLAINS OF COLORADO, trees were far too precious to be cut down and used to build houses. A traveler could look in all directions and count the number of trees on the horizon on the fingers of one hand. Early homesteaders proudly described their farms as having one tree or two, and if a family was lucky enough to have a tree, it was far more likely to build a house beneath the branches than to cut it down for building material. Even if settlers had preferred log cabins, they would have had to travel a prohibitive number of miles in every direction to find enough trees for even the smallest dwellings.

Colorado's first plains settlers used the next best building mate-

Walsenburg. At one time entire villages in southern Colorado were filled with flat-roofed pueblo-style houses made of adobe bricks. *Courtesy Colorado Historical Society.*

Starkville. Adobe bricks were inexpensive, and they made a dwelling that stayed warm in winter and cool in summer. *Kendal Atchison*

rial and built their homes from the earth, constructing dugouts, adobes, and soddies. Dugouts generally were temporary dwellings, usually little more than caves scooped out of the hillsides and fitted with doors and stovepipes. Sometimes families dug holes in the ground and covered them with boards or wagon covers, making a more permanent half-dugout.

No one lived in a dugout for long. This was not true for adobe and sod houses, however. When properly built, they were as snug as log cabins, and if maintained, they lasted almost as long. Although they had considerable drawbacks—for the most part, they were nearly impossible to keep clean—they were warm in the winter and cool in the summer and often were more comfortable than the frame houses that replaced them.

Adobes and soddies had another advantage: They were dirt cheap. The homeowner could build the house himself and only have to buy lumber for window and door frames and a pane or two of glass, an extravagance not everyone could afford. No nails were needed.

For the most part, these earthen houses were squat and simple squares with a single door and one or two windows. On occasion, however, adobe blocks were used to build large houses and even forts. Both Bent's Old Fort, a privately owned commercial structure near LaJunta, built by William Bent in 1833, and Fort Garland, operated by the military, were constructed of

Trim was painted a contrasting color, usually blue. *Kendal Atchison*

23

Antonito. Adobe relic. *Sandra Dallas*

Walsenburg. In time, stucco replaced mud-plaster, and owners added Victorian trim and pitched roofs to update flat-roofed adobe houses. *Kendal Atchison*

24

Keota. Adobe plaster was used on this "prairie box" house in Keota, where author James A. Michener gathered material for his epic, *Centennial. Sandra Dallas*

West of **Trinidad.** Properly made, adobe bricks were hard as concrete and strong enough to be used in large homes. *Courtesy Denver Public Library Western History Department.*

Trinidad. Richens Lacy ("Uncle Dick") Wootton ran a toll station on Raton Pass and earned lasting fame as the first merchant to ship the potent liquor Taos Lightning to Denver, in time for Christmas, 1858. His two-story adobe house is New Mexico territorial style. *Courtesy Colorado Historical Society.*

Conejos. A long adobe house has been made stylish with the addition of a gingerbread-trimmed porch and a stone balustrade. *Sandra Dallas*

Trinidad. Built in 1869 and purchased the following year by wealthy sheep rancher Don Felipe Baca, the Baca House is a blend of adobe construction and Victorian embellishments. The interior has been restored to replicate a prosperous Hispanic home of the 1870s. (Now a museum) *Sandra Dallas*

adobe. Strips of sod were used not only for entire communities of houses—Sterling had twenty-five—but also for churches and schools.

Early settlers learned to build adobe houses from the New Mexicans, many of whom moved to Colorado from Taos and other northern New Mexico settlements, bringing with them their knowledge of how to make sun-dried adobe bricks and smooth them with mud-plaster. All along the New Mexico border, in San Luis, Trinidad, and other settlements, towns were built of adobe.

Making adobe bricks required a certain amount of skill. When it reconstructed Bent's Old Fort in the mid-1970s, the National Park Service determined the best bricks were made with one part clay to three parts sand. Water constituted only 4 percent of the brick mixture, and straw or cheap Mexican wool was mixed in to add strength and allow for better curing. Properly made, the bricks were as strong as concrete blocks.

To prevent the bricks from eroding and melting back into the earth, adobe walls were covered with several layers of thin mud, smoothed on by hand and generally replastered every year. Over the years, cement replaced the mud-plaster, eliminating the annual need for maintenance though destroying the smooth patina.

27

Brush. Despite its traditional pueblo-style shape, this structure was built of adobe bricks in the early 1960s. *Sandra Dallas*

Greeley. Nathan Meeker, who founded Greeley in 1870, built his home of huge adobe blocks painted yellow. Adobe bricks, he wrote, "serve better than burned brick, and the walls are not so likely to crack, while they are much cheaper." *Kendal Atchison*

Fort Garland. The infantry barracks at Fort Garland were constructed of adobe with sod roofs. The mud-plastered interiors were whitewashed with lime and had wooden floors and adobe fireplaces. (Now a museum) *Kendal Atchison*

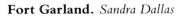

Fort Garland. *Sandra Dallas*

29

Bent's Old Fort. A medieval fortress with two bastions, Bent's Old Fort was a community built of adobe bricks and surrounded by adobe walls. Some sixty workers were employed as servants, blacksmiths, carpenters, clerks, and laborers by William Bent at the fort's prime in the 1840s. Cactus was planted on top of the walls to make them difficult to scale. The fort was rebuilt in the 1970s. (Now a museum) *Sandra Dallas*

Despite the adobe walls, which one visitor called "abominably cheerless," St. Vrain's Quarters, named for Bent's partner Cèran St. Vrain, were elegant compared to many of the bedrooms at the fort. Its occupants slept in a bed, rather than on straw pallets on adobe floors. *Sandra Dallas*

Interior walls were plastered with mud too, then often whitewashed with lime. A calico wainscoting was sometimes glued to the walls to keep the lime from rubbing off. Fireplaces, usually of a beehive shape and built into the corners of the rooms, provided heat.

Susan Shelby Magoffin, who visited Bent's Old Fort in 1846 with her husband, a Santa Fe trader, noted in her journal that the floors were sprinkled with water several times a day to keep down the dust and that in one large parlor or council room, a bucket of water and a cup were kept on a table for visitors, and "any water that may be left in the cup after drinking is unceremoniously tossed onto the floor."

Adobe buildings were confined mostly to southern Colorado. Farther north, sod strips were used. Settlers there, for the most part, did not know how to make adobe, and many were from Nebraska or Kansas where soddies or "Nebraska marble" houses were common. They were easy to build and involved little expense, but almost as important, they were comfortable. Many sod-busting families on the northeast plains owed their lives to the thick sod walls that kept out the cold during treacherous blizzards.

The site for a soddy required little preparation. Generally, the grass was removed, gopher holes filled in, and the ground tamped hard with a fence post. Using a sod-breaking plow, the farmer sliced out a section of prairie sod two to four inches thick, twelve to fourteen inches wide, and two to three feet long. Big bluestem or buffalo grasses were preferable and were best when cut in the fall when the grass was dry and wiry.

A door frame was positioned and then the sod blocks were laid around it two or three rows wide. Joints were staggered to prevent the wind from blowing through. Every third or fourth layer of sod was placed crosswise to bind the rows, and fine sand or mud was sifted into crevices to make them airtight. As the walls rose, window frames were set in. The roofs might be made of lumber, but often sod was used there too. Homesteaders sometimes added a landscaping touch by planting sunflowers on the roofs.

Soddies were snug and provided shelter from the heat of prairie

Susan Shelby Magoffin, wife of a Santa Fe trader, gave birth to a stillborn child in her room, upper right, at Bent's Old Fort in 1846. *Sandra Dallas*

East of **Security.** John R. Bradley selected the pueblo style for the elegant house that graced his prairie ranch. The 1927 house also was a gathering place for wealthy Colorado Springs swells who played polo nearby. In 1930 the house became the Fountain Valley School. *Laura Gilpin photograph courtesy of Fountain Valley School.*

31

Denver. In the World War I era, there was a surge of interest in Southwest Indian arts and crafts as well as in the pueblo-style architecture. Twentieth-century adobes were a far cry from the mud-plastered houses of the past. This flat-roofed house with protruding *vigas* (log beams), built in 1917, is in Denver's exclusive Country Club area. *Sandra Dallas*

West of **Weldona.** To prevent deterioration and keep dirt from flaking down into the rooms, many sod houses were coated inside and out with plaster or stucco. *Sandra Dallas*

Aurora. Sod was used to recreate this 1888 farmhouse, copied from a Yuma County home, at the Plains Conservation Center. The center also has a sod barn and a sod schoolhouse. *Sandra Dallas*

summers and the cold and wind of winter blizzards, but that was the most that could be said for them. Sand and soil continuously sifted down from the ceiling onto inhabitants and everything else in the room, including food. During rainstorms, trickles of dirty water leaked through the roofs and walls, particularly if the joints were not alternated properly. Insects made their way through the sod, and one woman remembered looking up from the supper table to see a snake gliding through the wall.

Like early adobe houses to the south, soddies were sparsely furnished, generally containing homemade tables and chairs and mattresses stuffed with prairie grasses. Occasionally a battered bureau or a factory-made dresser, hauled across the prairie from wherever home had been, stood in the corner. There might be a trunk that doubled as a seat, within which were stored silk dresses. The dresses were taken out and lovingly admired, then refolded and put away. They were rarely worn. If the housewife was affluent, she covered the walls and ceiling with muslin or calico and filled the deep windows with geraniums or vines.

Sometimes, as lumber became available, the settlers erected frame walls inside and outside the soddy, turning the sod layers

Layers of sod were cut two to four inches thick. The tough dry grass gripped the layers next to it like interlocking wires. *Sandra Dallas*

33

West of **Orchard.** Sod was not as stable a building material as adobe, and
this two-story house is rare. *Sandra Dallas*

into insulation. More often, they deserted the soddy for a frame
house and turned the old sod structure into a barn or a chicken
coop; sometimes a soddy merely melted into the ground.

3. Mountain Jigsaw

Log cabins served well enough for the first frenzied gold seekers who rushed to each new strike. But they were hardly the style of architecture the new boomers, who inevitably followed the prospectors, wanted to see in their towns. These promoters and speculators dressed their towns in euphemisms, pretentiously calling a collection of mud-chinked cabins on a rutted trail a "city." Colorado is replete with ghost towns like Parrot City, Engineer City, and Capitol City, all of them marked by a few rotting logs and a handful of ghosts.

"Making governments and building towns are the natural employments of the migratory Yankee," wrote Albert D. Richardson, who came west with famed *New York Tribune* editor Horace Greeley. "Congregate a hundred Americans anywhere beyond the settlements, and they immediately lay out a city, frame a state con-

LaJunta. Carpenter Gothic houses took their basic design from the center-gable frame, stone, and brick farmhouses popular in the Middle West. *Sandra Dallas*

Canon City. Harriet and Anson Rudd built this ten-room stone house about 1880 and lived in it until 1904. The rooms were small and cramped, and the bathroom was so cold it was turned into a storeroom for milk and butter. Rudd was a blacksmith, a civic leader, and a poet. (Now a museum) *Kendal Atchison*

South of **Gold Hill.** The gable carried to extreme. *Sandra Dallas*

Gold Hill. Most frame houses were built with lap siding, but on occasion boards and battens were used. The battens were placed over seams where the boards came together to keep out the cold. *Sandra Dallas*

Silver Plume. The center gable is an ornamental feature of many carpenter Gothic houses. *Sandra Dallas*

37

Central City. Many mountain homebuilders were required to be not only architects but engineers and sometimes magicians, cramming houses onto narrow lots on steep mountainsides. *Courtesy Denver Public Library Western History Department.*

stitution and apply for admission into the Union, while twenty-five of them become candidates for the United States Senate."

Town boomers, along with home-starved women who longed for the little frame cottages they had left behind, were a powerful force in turning wagon ruts into roads and replacing log cabins with civilized houses. Denver was only a few months old when Richardson noted that "frame and brick edifices were displacing mud-roofed log cabins."

They were not much by outside standards, but in Colorado they were castles. "In New York, our one-story house, fourteen feet by twenty with eight feet of shed for a kitchen, would be an indifferent stable; here it is a palace. Walls of rough upright boards, with cracks battened to keep out rain and dust . . . a square, clapboard front, three doors, three windows, and a stove-pipe protruding from the kitchen-roof. It cost three hundred dollars . . . what more could human nature ask?" Richardson wrote.

Denver. By the early 1860s, Denver had replaced log cabins with frame houses whose simple lines were even then softened by gingerbread trim, which also decorated outhouses. *Courtesy Colorado Historical Society.*

What more, indeed. Richardson may have been content in his drafty board cottage with the protruding stovepipe, but few of the women who followed their gold-crazed husbands west would settle for that. This was the onset of the Victorian era in which home—women's sphere—was all important. The Victorians loved everything about the home; after all, they popularized central heating, indoor plumbing, lawn mowers, and antimacassars.

Homeowners were admonished by architectural writers such as Andrew Jackson Downing to express themselves in their home designs. "Man naturally desires to give some distinctive character to his own habitation, to mark its superiority to those devoted to animals," Downing wrote. Colorado's early settlers took seriously the views expressed by Downing and others, and barely had the first frame houses replaced log cabins than they were enlarged and decorated with gingerbread trim, painted in the latest colors, and planted with scraggly grass and vines.

Colorado's first distinctive architecture was carpenter Gothic. It

39

Fraser. Beneath most carpenter Gothic dwellings was a simple, prosaic structure. *Kendal Atchison*

Leadville. Little different in size and shape from the Fraser house is this Leadville confection where every corner and flat surface has been adorned with gingerbread trim. *Courtesy Colorado Historical Society.*

was based on the stern, gabled stone or brick farmhouses of the Middle West, which in turn were copied after the solid medieval castles and churches of Europe. When translated into wood, Gothic architecture became a distinctive style known as American Gothic or carpenter Gothic.

Colorado carpenters initially used simple Gothic designs, but they soon became bored with this and began to experiment with their jigsaws, icing the houses they built with intricately carved trim and decorating the barns and privies as well. Most of this architecture was in the mining camps because the miners' strike-it-rich attitudes called for ostentation. In addition, because taste was never much of a factor in early domestic architecture in Colorado, early builders turned out a lavish style of mountain jigsaw architecture that even today symbolizes the dreams of the early prospectors. Regardless of the style or size of the house—most carpenter Gothic houses were small with poorly planned room arrangements—it could be decorated on gables or eaves or front porches with fanciful trim.

Leadville. This Gothic home with its restrained trim was respectable enough for a storekeeper and town mayor, but H. A. W. Tabor was quick to desert it for a mansion in Denver after he struck silver. Augusta Tabor was made of sterner stuff and found the Leadville house, once she rid herself of the boarders she kept for years, could be more comfortable than the Denver home. *Author's Collection.*

Leadville. Years later, Tabor's impoverished second wife, Baby Doe, who moved back to Leadville after her husband died, was evicted from this house for nonpayment of rent. *Sandra Dallas*

41

Victor. In Cripple Creek and Victor, houses were built into the mountainsides. Long stairways led to the front doors. *Kendal Atchison*

Crested Butte. Sheds or small houses were often tacked onto a house to enlarge it. *Sandra Dallas*

Lake City. Suitably Gothic, this house was the first parsonage built on Colorado's western slope. *Sandra Dallas*

Silverton. Gothic apparently was the style of choice at other western slope parsonages. *Sandra Dallas*

43

Leadville. While stained and leaded glass generally were used to show off affluence, the window in Leadville's "House with the Eye," built in the 1880s, was chauvinistic; Its owner copied the stained glass eye from the eye in Colorado's state seal. (Now a museum) *Kendal Atchison*

Leadville. Toward the end of the mountain jigsaw period, builders turned to mass production, which in those days meant two or three houses, not dozens. Different color schemes gave them individuality. *Kendal Atchison*

Georgetown (*above*) and **Aspen** (*below*). One-story mountain jigsaw houses kept the lines of their statelier two-story cousins with steep gables often bisected by crossbars, and long, narrow windows. The L-shape house, which allowed for a covered front porch, was a popular design. *Courtesy Denver Public Library Western History Department* (*above*); *Kendal Atchison* (*below*)

45

Builders did not spend all their time on exterior decoration, however. They were called on to be tricksters as well, because the houses often were squeezed between prospect holes or built on steep mountainsides. Nineteenth-century historian Frank Hall described one mining town as "a bleak and wholly uninviting region, where is not to be found a space sufficiently level to serve as a site for even a small circus tent, or an eligible cemetery; not a tree, shrub, flower, or grass plot to relieve the tiresome monotony of brown rocks and verdueless soil; where the hillsides are pitted." Here, he noted, "rows of cheap and ugly frame buildings were held up in dizzy heights on stilts along the densely populated ravines."

In Central City, observed Bert McFarland in a prospectus for a local mine, houses were built on mountainsides so steep that the roof of one could be on a level with the foundation of the one above it. "It is said that the man living the furthest uptown in

Pueblo. In 1883–84, as he became more prosperous, James N. Carlile, politician, railroad contractor, real estate promoter, and empire builder, dressed up his plain, ten-year-old Gothic house with a porch, gingerbread trim, and a sweeping veranda. He added marble fireplaces, frescoed ceilings, and even window screens. Poor Carlile. A decade later, when the 1893 crash hit, he had to scrap plans for a mansion like those built by other Pueblo titans. He died in 1921, still living in the cottage. *Sandra Dallas*

Georgetown. With their steep roofs and barnlike demeanor, Gothic houses were impressive on the outside but often cold, drafty, and expensive to heat. *Courtesy Denver Public Library Western History Department.*

Colorado Springs. Author Helen Hunt Jackson moved to Colorado Springs for her health in 1873. She not only recovered but found a husband, who presented her with this cottage, which had been built by Cripple Creek's first millionaire, Winfield Scott Stratton, while he was still a carpenter. Jackson wrote *Ramona* while living here. *Courtesy Colorado Historical Society.*

47

Denver. Most of Denver's frame houses are gone, replaced under a city ordinance that requires brick or stone. This rare example of carpenter Gothic in Denver has been updated with a bay of Italianate windows. *Sandra Dallas*

Leadville. Jigsaw carving could dress up the dreariest house, which was why carpenter Gothic was sometimes referred to as "false fronts and Mary Ann behinds." *Kendal Atchison*

Central City empties his ashes down the smoke stack of the house adjoining, which process is carried along in turn by everyone . . . the resident at the foot of the hill dumping the ashes of the entire town into the creek."

Central City was not unique. In Victor, for example, author Anne Ellis lived in a two-room frame house that was built into the mountainside. "To get in the front room, one had to climb a flight of twelve or fifteen rickety steps, while the back door was even with the ground," she wrote.

Inside, because furnishings were now easier to come by than in the log cabin days, houses were furnished with as much style as the owner could afford. In remote areas, the choice was still meager, however. Harriet Fish Backus, who lived high above Telluride at the Tomboy Mine shortly after the turn of the century, moved from one shack to another because its privy was closer to the house, eliminating hours of snow shoveling in the winter.

"It was customary for those leaving the hill to sell their meager furniture to the new occupants," she wrote. Mrs. Backus and her

Central City. Gingerbread trim, lace curtains, and a yard planted with baby's breath gave a delicate look to this Gothic house. *Kendal Atchison*

Georgetown. Every carpenter Gothic house was different. Board-and-batten siding and square windows with muntin bars give variation to this highly decorated house. *Courtesy Denver Public Library Western History Department.*

Silverton. Mining camp gingerbread. *Sandra Dallas*

Salida. Gray Cottage, with its steamboat Gothic air, was built in 1882 by G. R. Gray, who operated the Madonna Mine west of Salida. At one time the finest house in Salida, it was sold for $1,800 in 1886 after Gray and his wife Julia were divorced. *Kendal Atchison*

Pineapples on the front porch are a southern symbol of hospitality. *Kendal Atchison*

51

Black Hawk. The Lace House, Colorado's best-known Victorian house, was built in 1863 by Lucien K. Smith and has had an unremarkable history. For years it stood deserted, giving rise to ghost stories. It was restored in 1976. (Now a Museum) *Kendal Atchison*

Central City. Prominent businessman Eben Smith erected a carpenter Gothic house similar to his cousin's Lace House in Black Hawk. *Kendal Atchison*

Buena Vista. Wooden carving around the windows and along the crest of the roof indicates the work of a fine craftsman. *Kendal Atchison*

Denver. Jigsaw architecture often spilled over into the cities. The house is more important than the people in this family portrait. *Author's Collection.*

53

Central City. Inside, the Thomas house is a museumlike collection of Victorian furnishings. Pillow covers on the brass bed in the master bedroom are embroidered "Good Night" and "Good Morning." *Sandra Dallas*

Central City. Greek revival architecture never was very popular in the Colorado mining towns, probably because it was too spartan. This house, built in the 1870s, was given to Marcia and Benjamin Prosser Thomas as a wedding gift in 1895 and has remained in the family ever since. Thomas was connected with the Sauer–McShane Mercantile Company, a major retail outlet. *Kendal Atchison*

husband paid $75 for a potbellied stove in their new parlor and a coal range in the kitchen, a mattress on legs, two chairs, one made of three twelve-inch boards painted black, a kitchen table and chairs, and three narrow shelves.

Anne Ellis was luckier when she moved into the Victor house. Her landlady, who owned a number of rental properties, furnished the house with a bright red velvet carpet. "I imagine she bought it for one of the cribs, then changed her mind," Ellis noted.

As their owners became more prosperous, the little mountain jigsaw houses began to fill up with wonders of the middle-class Victorian era. These were typically velvet draperies and table spreads, dried flowers and dead birds preserved under glass domes, matching sets of furniture crammed into tiny rooms, pictures of European mountain scenes and portraits of family members (a fa-

54

vorite was a photograph of one's dead child, artfully posed by the undertaker), handpainted china and lamps, and all kinds of mining accoutrements, from ore samples to miners' candlesticks.

The suffocating array of furnishings and overblown exteriors finally crumbled under its own weight. The Victorian era and its carpenter Gothic architecture became too fusty and old-fashioned, and as America moved into the twentieth century, mountain jigsaw architecture fell into disrepute. It survived because the towns gave out about the time the style did, and there was no money to replace or remodel the houses—to the relief of nouveau Victorians who today prize carpenter Gothic above all other Colorado domestic architectural styles.

Central City. Calendars from Sauer–McShane hang in the bathroom. *Sandra Dallas*

Aspen. Gingerbread houses were as elaborate inside as out. Housewives were challenged to let no space go unadorned. *Courtesy Denver Public Library Western History Department.*

55

Georgetown. Georgetown grocer Virgil B. Potter built a gloriously Victorian addition to his tiny frame house after a lucky grubstake. The house, copied from a design book, is a vocabulary of Victorian architecture inside and out—mansard roof, cupola, Italianate windows, stained glass, fancy siding, grained wood, and ornate gaslight fixtures. After Potter lost his money in the 1893 silver crash, the house was acquired by Frank A. Maxwell, who designed the unique railroad "loop" connecting Georgetown with Silver Plume. Maxwell House was once designated one of the ten best examples of Victorian houses in the country by the American Institute of Architects. *Sandra Dallas*

Georgetown. General William A. Hamill took a simple Gothic cottage and turned it into a mansion with a solarium and collection of outbuildings. Inside, the restored house is awash in flowered carpets and blue, gold, and brown flowered wallpaper. Floors are alternating stripes of walnut and maple, and there are polished shutters and heavy draperies at the windows. After the Hamill family sold the house in 1915, it was first a boardinghouse and later a private museum. Georgetown Society, Incorporated acquired Hamill House in 1970 and has spent $500,000 on restoration. (Now a museum) *Sandra Dallas*

General Hamill built a stone stable and stone office building behind his house but failed to complete them after he lost his money in the 1893 silver crash. The stable is topped by a dovecote. *Sandra Dallas*

While Hamill House had running water inside, the family relied on an outside privy. This one had three walnut seats for use by the family, three pine seats for their servants. Georgetown Society workers excavated the long unused privy vault during restoration to find hundreds of medicine bottles and bits of broken china, thrown there by servants to hide their clumsiness. *Sandra Dallas*

Denver. Phrenologist and sex educator Orson Fowler designed the octagon house in the 1850s and touted its exceptional use of space, claiming eight sides meant more sunlight and better communication between rooms than with the standard rectangle. The idea caught on with some radicals, such as feminist and dress reformer Amelia Bloomer, but died out after the Civil War. Octagon houses west of the Mississippi are rare. While this house, built in 1876, actually is rectangular, it is dominated by its octagon tower. *Sandra Dallas*

Telluride. This nouveau-Victorian conglomeration, copied after the charming mountain jigsaw cottages of the past, belongs to actress Susan Saint James. *Sandra Dallas*

4. Romantic Victorian

WHEN IT APPEARED that many of the boomtowns would live on, that the economy could support a permanent population, and that Colorado might even become a state, Coloradans turned to the task of building cities. It was no small undertaking, Jerome C. Smiley related in his *History of Denver.* Like other Colorado towns, Denver "was not a pretty place," wrote Smiley, adding: "its motley, irregular, ugly structures . . . were calculated to cause nightmare in the brain of an unseasoned visi-

Boulder. The whole neighborhood showed up when the photographer took a picture of L. Cheney's home. The house is a transitional Italianate, Gothic in shape but with Italian windows. Shutters are a touch of villa architecture. *Courtesy Colorado Historical Society.*

Boulder. The belvedere in the center of the roof was an architectural device transplanted from the Atlantic Coast where it served as a ship lookout. *Courtesy Denver Public Library Western History Department.*

Georgetown. The widow's walk was also an eastern architectural embellishment. This one probably was unused, because it is unlikely there was an attic access to the roof. Hamill House is next door (see pages 56–57). Wooden frames at the edge of the plank sidewalk kept horses from eating the saplings. *Courtesy Denver Public Library Western History Department.*

tor. It is probable that nowhere else in the world were ever seen such architectural horrors."

Town fathers undertook the building of cities with the same determination that they had applied earlier to carving settlements out of the wilderness. They graded and then paved the streets of their towns, laid stones for sidewalks, installed street lamps, and erected fine schools and courthouses and churches.

Civic pride required a new style of domestic architecture to go with the fine new cities, one that stressed romance and sophistication, one more refined than the hit-or-miss carpenter Gothic that swept the early towns. Never very confident about their own judgment, Colorado architects turned to the eastern United States for inspiration. No matter that the styles they selected had been around for fifty years. They were new to Colorado. It was far more important that these styles exuded refinement and grace and on occasion even good taste.

The most popular of these imported romantic styles were Italianate and Second Empire or mansard. Italianate architecture—

also known as Tuscan, villa, and Lombard—was borrowed from rural and northern Italy and was enormously popular in the eastern part of the country after early architectural guru Andrew Jackson Downing promoted its use in small houses.

Italianate featured low roofs with overhangs that were held up by elaborate brackets. Delicate pilasters supported decorative porches, and the corners of the houses often were outlined in quoins. Italianate houses nearly always had long, narrow, round-topped windows, which gave a gracious, open look, a real advance for Coloradans who were only a few years away from the threat of Indian attacks. Such houses could be rendered in brick, stone, or even wood; some of the most imaginative were built by skilled carpenters who turned their mountain jigsaw skills to making intricate brackets and even wooden quoins for these sophisticated villas.

Even more popular than the Italianate was the Second Empire style, which had its heyday in the 1860s in France during the reign

The same house has been painted to emphasize architectural details. *Kendal Atchison*

Idaho Springs. In a follow-up to carpenter Gothic, builders continued to copy stone details in wood. Quoins, popular in eastern Italianate houses, are rendered in wood. *Kendal Atchison*

Lawson. Wooden quoins were popular in the towns along Clear Creek and gave architectural style to the simplest houses. *Kendal Atchison*

Denver. Curtis Park, a near-downtown neighborhood now undergoing major restoration, was in its prime during the Italianate period. These brick villas with their long, narrow windows, carved stone lintels, paneled doors, and fancifully carved brackets and porch posts were the height of sophistication. *Sandra Dallas*

63

Greeley. A rare Colorado example of frame Italianate shows off elaborate brackets and delicately turned porch posts. *Kendal Atchison*

of Napoleon III. The style incorporated many Italianate features, such as tall windows and small porches, but its most distinctive feature was the mansard roof. Originally used in the seventeenth century in France, the mansard is a double-pitched roof with a steep bottom slope that turns the attic into a full-scale story. The mansard was especially appealing because it could be mixed with other architectural styles in a mansion or be used as the primary architectural feature in a cottage.

Central City. The mansard was the most popular feature of Colorado Victorian architecture. *Sandra Dallas*

Mancos. The town of Mancos grew up around the 1890 George Bauer mansion, which once was the center of a prosperous farm. Before he established a bank, Bauer, who was mayor of Mancos in 1894, kept his money behind a loose brick near the fireplace. The house also was once a hospital and later was divided into apartments. *Sandra Dallas*

65

Manitou Springs. The mansard could be used on a stylish house like this one with fanciful wood siding, rusticated stone, and stone quoins. *Kendal Atchison*

East of **Garfield.** There is an air of mystery to this deserted romantic. *Sandra Dallas*

Denver. When Stephen Knight, a bookkeeper at Eagle Milling and Elevator Company, married Kate Davis, his boss's daughter, her parents built them this mansard house. Knight did well, rising to manager of the company. The house has done well, too. As part of Ninth Street Park, it was restored by Historic Denver, Incorporated. *Sandra Dallas*

Denver. The mansard could be combined with any detail of Victorian architecture, such as elaborate pediments above the windows, gingerbread brackets, even an iron widow's walk. *Courtesy Denver Public Library Western History Department.*

67

Aspen. An air of mystery surrounds Pioneer Park, this 1880s house built by Aspen Mayor Henry Webber, whose first wife died under mysterious circumstances. Legend says he tried to murder his second wife on the stairway of the house. In later years the house was owned by Walter P. Paepcke, head of the Aspen Institute for Humanistic Studies, who was responsible in part for Aspen's post–World War II revival. *Sandra Dallas*

Canon City. A pseudo-mansard tops this two-story house. Farmhouse shutters disguise the Italianate windows. *Sandra Dallas*

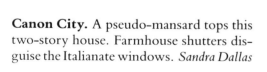

Salida. Another mock mansard gives a formal air to an otherwise barnlike house. Next door is Gray Cottage (see page 51). *Courtesy Denver Public Library Western History Department.*

Silverton. This mansard is a dictionary of wood-carving art. *Sandra Dallas*

69

Salida. This mansard bisects the second floor. *Kendal Atchison*

Aspen. Built by a druggist, this Aspen mansard later became famous as the home of Luke Short, the well-known author of western novels. *Sandra Dallas*

Buena Vista. Windows installed in mansard roofs could be of any style or shape. These round-top Italianate windows are covered by elaborate gingerbread designs. *Kendal Atchison*

Victor. The mansard was equally at home on a plain frame house. *Kendal Atchison*

Denver. Charles Chever, the first clerk and recorder for Arapahoe County (which at that time included Denver), arrived in Colorado in 1861 and made a fortune in real estate. Had he lived long enough, he would have made a second fortune on his mansard house, because it is located on prime downtown Denver land. *Courtesy Denver Public Library Western History Department.*

There was another Second Empire feature that Coloradans embraced, as did Victorians all over the country, and that was the cupola, a spire almost always topped by a tiny mansard roof and punctured with bull's eye or other decorative windows. Even though the inside of the cupola was often nothing more than storage space, the exterior was stunning, making the exquisite little tower the most distinctive feature of Victorian architecture in America. Coloradans used it to turn any small house into a miniature castle.

The romantic Victorians were long-lived. The Italianate turned itself into the ubiquitous Denver square, while the mansard still is a popular feature in suburban homes. The cupola, of course, lives on, in a thousand horror movies, paintings, and stories as a symbol of the once elegant and sometimes wicked Victorian era.

Denver. Victorian architects frequently got carried away. The cupola, useless except as a decoration, dominates this cottage. (No longer in existence) *Sandra Dallas*

Leadville. George E. King was so enamored with mansards that he used them on his house and on the Tabor Grand Hotel and the Delaware Block, which he designed in downtown Leadville. The tiny mansard on the porch roof is painted in green stripes. *Kendal Atchison*

73

Boulder. The architect of this house seems to have used every Victorian architectural feature he could think of—cupola, bull's-eye windows, iron grill-work, gingerbread bargeboards, brackets, porch posts, banisters, and bay window. *Courtesy Denver Public Library Western History Department.*

Trinidad. Cattleman Frank G. Bloom built Colorado's most elaborate Second Empire house from a pattern book. The house has sixteen-foot ceilings, though its rooms are conventional sizes, and there is only one staircase. Bloom, who lived in the house nearly fifty years, was one of the state's most powerful men. He opened a trading post in Colorado in the 1860s with the Thatcher brothers, who later founded a southern Colorado banking empire. Bloom married their sister, and his own daughter married into the Iliff family of legendary western cattle ranchers. *Sandra Dallas*

"A Merry Heart Maketh a Cheerful Countenance." *Sandra Dallas*

75

Denver. Second Empire quoins are evident on this neoclassical revival house. It was built by mining and banking magnate Eben Smith, who left Colorado a classic carpenter Gothic house in Central City (see page 52). *Sandra Dallas*

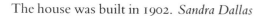

The house was built in 1902. *Sandra Dallas*

Denver. M. M. ("Brick") Pomeroy was a flamboyant dreamer and promoter whose schemes ran from gold mines to a railroad tunnel under the Continental Divide, which never got farther than a few feet into the mountain near Loveland Pass. His elaborate Second Empire house in Denver's Highlands area included a mineral gallery for ore specimens and a brick hen house. The home, known as "Pomeroy's Folly," was as ephemeral as his promotions and was torn down in the 1930s. *Courtesy Denver Public Library Western History Department.*

5. Late Victorian

COLORADO CAME OF AGE in the late Victorian era, and Coloradans with money and a desire to spend it on houses chose from a bewildering array of domestic architectural styles—Queen Anne, shingle, "stick," Eastlake, Georgian, or, more often, a combination of several or all of the above. Ernest Ingersoll, who wrote travel books that were sold by the railroads, visited Denver in the 1880s and noted: "Homes succeed one another in endlessly varying styles of architecture."

Aspen. The favorite housing style of Aspen white-collar workers was this small cottage with its Eastlake bay window. During Aspen's post–World War II revival, many were painted in pastel pink and yellow, but in recent years they have been repainted in multicolored San Francisco hues. *Kendal Atchison*

Aspen. While the vertical siding is a later addition, it is similar to board–and–batten siding used by early miners. *Kendal Atchison*

South of **Leadville.** A pair of bay windows relieve this elongated ranch house. *Kendal Atchison*

Breckenridge. Double-deck Eastlake windows make this two-story log cabin fashionable. *Sandra Dallas*

Fort Collins. As machine-made trim replaced scroll-sawn carpenter work, structures such as this 1880s house blossomed with "cannonball" porch posts, spoolwork, and cut shingles. *Kendal Atchison*

Telluride (*above*); **Boulder** (*below*). Any house could be dressed up with an Eastlake porch. *Sandra Dallas* (*top photo*), *Kendal Atchison* (*bottom photo*)

Boulder. What schoolgirl would not be proud to be framed by this dramatic porch? *Courtesy Denver Public Library Western History Department.*

Boulder. The late Victorians did tortuous things with wood, bending it into fantastic shapes for railings and furniture. *Courtesy Denver Public Library Western History Department.*

Boulder. These houses are a catalog of woodworking genius. *Courtesy Denver Public Library Western History Department.*

83

Salida. Exterior clutter was repeated inside to an extreme. *Courtesy Denver Public Library Western History Department.*

Denver. This serene grandmother is at odds with the busy clutter of dozens of patterns on rugs, fabrics, wallpaper, and knickknacks. *Author's Collection.*

Georgetown. John Henry Bowman, a prosperous mining man, built the comfortable Bowman-White house for his family in 1892, and his daughter, Mellie Bowman White lived there until 1974. The house has a "coffin" door, so-called because it was used only for funerals and other formal occasions, and "dragon-back" trim on the roof, properly called roof combing. (Now a museum) *Courtesy Colorado Historical Society.*

Fairplay. James Marshall Paul commuted from this American barnlike house on the hill in Fairplay over Mosquito Pass to his Printer Boy Mine in Leadville. Originally the house had a stone wall in front with a long stairway leading to the street. At the back of the house there was a stable and a tennis court. *Sandra Dallas*

85

Buena Vista. Stick houses featured boards nailed on the finished house in vertical, horizontal, or even diagonal patterns. This brooding, unpainted relic is a hulking counterpart to the more romantic mansard across the street. *Kendal Atchison*

As gold and silver poured out of the mountains, Colorado cities went on a building binge. In a period of only six years, as Jerome C. Smiley related in his *History of Denver,* virtually all of Denver's nineteenth-century commercial structures were built, and at the same time thousands of houses were erected. By 1893, he wrote, "There were literally miles of these dwellings erected during that extraordinary period." Noted architects, either from Denver or the East, were commissioned to design stylish cottages or mansions that were testaments to wealth. Now better educated, Coloradans were more knowledgeable about architecture and were no longer dependent on the tastes of local builders. If they had the means, they could ride the palace cars to Chicago and New York for architectural inspiration, and some even sailed to Europe to gather ideas and furnishings for their new homes.

More than ever, a home became a personal statement. Quantity was more important than quality, and ostentation was most important of all. Certain styles prevailed. Greek revival was popular

Crested Butte. Built in the 1980s, these nouveau-mountain Gothic houses have the gaunt look of a century ago. *Sandra Dallas*

Silverton. Gustav Stoiber, wealthy silver mine owner, lived in this once elegant mansion. *Sandra Dallas*

87

because of its enormous columns. Eastlake was a sort of updated carpenter Gothic with machine-turned porch spindles, often with knobs on them. The "stick" style featured frame siding outlined geometrically with diagonal or upright sticks or lathes. Shingle style, copied after the great, overblown cottages of eastern resorts, could be almost any style covered with wooden shingles. It was especially popular in Colorado Springs, which attracted vacationing or ailing Easterners. Many who came to Colorado were suffering from tuberculosis and believed the dry mountain air would cure them.

The most favored style was Queen Anne, because it encompassed almost everything—gables, towers, shingled second stories, towering chimneys, sharp roofs. Queen Anne–style houses could be constructed of just about any building material. Queen Anne also included an endless variety of porches, which were "well occupied during the long, cool twilight," Ingersoll observed.

The Queen Anne and other styles could be painted any color

Pueblo. This geometric structure, built by ice dealer E. D. Olin about 1890, is built with five half-octagons. *Sandra Dallas*

Colorado Springs (*top and center*); **Canon City** (*below*). This shingle style was so called because either the whole house or at least its upper stories were covered by shingles. *Kendal Atchison* (*top photo*); *Sandra Dallas* (*center photo*); *Kendal Atchison* (*bottom photo*)

Denver. Jesse Welborn, president of Colorado Fuel and Iron Company, built this home on his country estate in the 1920s. Today, it is part of Colorado Academy. *Sandra Dallas*

Denver. This shingled gardenhouse sits behind the enormous stone Fitzroy Place (see page 125). *Sandra Dallas*

except white. Andrew Jackson Downing decreed that houses *never* should be white, which, he said, was "entirely unsuitable and in bad taste." At first Coloradans ignored him, but in 1870 the *Rocky Mountain News* commented on the ghastly number of white houses, "an overpowering and repulsive color." It recommended a neutral tint for the body of a house and a lighter or darker shade of the same color for the trim. By the end of the century Coloradans were taking Downing's and the *News's* advice, and their houses blossomed forth in cream and tan and yellow, as well as those Victorian favorites, dark green, dark brown, and maroon.

There was no distinctive Colorado style during the late Victorian era. "Western architects are not restricted to one or two models in the construction of houses," noted *The Western Architect & Building News*. "For this reason a residence street in a Western city does not present the monotonous appearance of some of the streets in the cities of the Far East."

There was, however, a certain conforming characteristic on the interiors—eclecticism. Clutter was the watchword within, whether the home was a mansion or a cottage, and it was inevi-

Boulder. Famed architect H. H. Richardson designed this house in the 1890s. With its hilltop setting and broad expanse of ground, it is reminiscent of vacation homes in eastern resorts. *Sandra Dallas*

Colorado Springs. Judson Moss Bemis, founder of the J. M. Bemis Company, which manufactured bags and other containers, built this house for his wife, who moved to Colorado Springs for her health. The 1885 house is now a bed-and-breakfast inn. *Kendal Atchison*

Manitou Springs. This shingle-style house has a spring in the basement.
Sandra Dallas

Redstone. Cleveholm was built by coal magnate John Cleveland Osgood to rival the summer cottages on the Atlantic Coast. Among his guests were John D. Rockefeller and Theodore Roosevelt. *Kendal Atchison*

Denver. This overblown cottage probably was built by William Lang, Denver's most popular architect. *Sandra Dallas*

94

Denver. Another William Lang design, this house is dominated by its dramatic stone arches. *Sandra Dallas*

Florence. Queen Anne was an all-purpose architecture that combined the remnants of the gingerbread era with the wonders of modern design. Its main features are dominant gables, towers, and a collection of porches. *Sandra Dallas*

Telluride. "Mountain Queen Anne." *Sandra Dallas*

Lake City. It can be difficult to tell where mountain jigsaw ends and Queen
Anne begins. *Sandra Dallas*

Cripple Creek. Charles N. Miller, one of ninety-one lawyers in Cripple Creek, built this fine house. It later belonged to Edward Bell, who was sheriff during Cripple Creek's labor wars. *Kendal Atchison*

Denver. Frederick W. Neef, a German brewer, let no surface go undecorated in his 1886 house. Even the fence has elaborate designs. *Sandra Dallas*

Palisade. There are elements of Queen Anne in this farmhouse. *Sandra Dallas*

Boulder. Mork from Ork, actor Robin Williams's irrepressible alien, lived in this house on the "Mork and Mindy" television series, which was set in Boulder. *Sandra Dallas*

Denver. A "Princess" Anne cottage. *Sandra Dallas*

Salida. Towers are a dominant feature of nineteenth-century Salida domestic architecture. *Courtesy Denver Public Library Western History Department.*

Pueblo. Gambler Charles E. Allison, who built this house about 1890, frequently used it as collateral for his bets. *Sandra Dallas*

Denver. Frank E. Edbrooke, who designed the Brown Palace Hotel and the Central Presbyterian Church, both in Denver, designed this slightly more modest structure as his home. *Sandra Dallas*

Denver. Typical of hundreds of mass-produced Queen Anne houses in Denver, this one gained fame because Buffalo Bill Cody died here in 1917. *Sandra Dallas*

Pueblo. One of several houses built in 1890 by speculator R. A. Thomas (and possibly lost by him in the 1893 silver crash), this Queen Anne was the home of prominent physician and mayor, A. L. Fugard. *Sandra Dallas*

The elaborate gable trim is similar to that of other **Pueblo** houses. *Sandra Dallas*

Denver. With its rusticated brick, the Tedford house, built in 1890, is part of a block-long collection of historic homes in the 1400 block of Vine Street.
Sandra Dallas

Gunnison. Rancher Alonzo Hartman built this tower-heavy house about 1894. The first floor of the tower has a white oak stairway; the turret was an artist's studio. The kitchen was in the basement.
Sandra Dallas

107

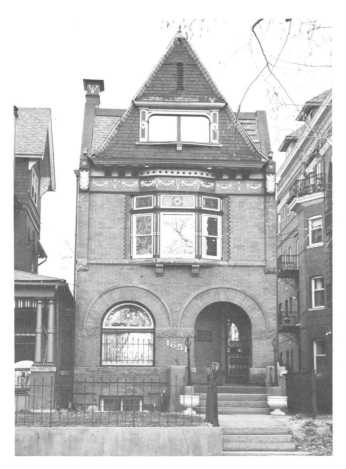 

Denver. Though they could be designed with the panache of mansions, townhouses were a rarity in Colorado.
Sandra Dallas

tably described as "tasteful," something it generally was not. The decor was what was sometimes called "General Grant" or "Pullman-car Gothic." It included floridly patterned carpets, pattern-on-pattern wallpapers, paisley shawls, brocade throws, and needlework pillows scattered on tufted fainting couches. The windows had to be shuttered and draped. A library table standing in the center of the room was a nice touch, as were potted palms and elaborate chandeliers. Bric-a-brac was prized; plaster statues, handpainted plates, photo and postcard albums, rugs woven by American Indians, collections of seashells, and anything Oriental were popular items.

The interiors of the smaller houses were still a series of cramped rooms, but the interiors of the larger homes reflected their owners' growing social ambitions. They had salons and conservatories, ballrooms and libraries, with vast amounts of waste space in enormous stairways and entrance halls and reception rooms. And, of course, there were coachmen's rooms and servants' quarters.

Denver. Poet Thomas Hornsby Ferril moved into this house as a boy in 1900. In his poems, Ferril writes about the huge water wagons that sprinkled Downing Street in front of the house, pulled by horses wearing sunbonnets and with golden knobs on their hames. *Sandra Dallas*

The smaller homes of the eclectic period survived as dwellings, and many remain private residences today. The mansions suffered a sadder fate. Always expensive to maintain, they grew increasingly costly to operate in the twentieth century, particularly as servants demanded decent wages. As the neighborhoods around the old mansions deteriorated, the houses were torn down to make way for commercial structures, or turned into boardinghouses and offices.

Many were divided into apartments. After World War II, famed novelist Jack Kerouac, who prowled the alleys of Denver with his friend Neal Cassidy (immortalized as Dean Moriarty), recalled visiting one Denver mansion that had fallen on hard times:

> Carlo's basement apartment was on Grant Street in an old red-brick rooming house near a church. You went down an alley, down some stone steps, opened an old raw door, and went through a kind of cellar till you came to his board door.*

For those mansions that survived, the future is considerably brighter. Many have been turned into condominiums and expensive office space.

*From *On the Road* by Jack Kerouac. Copyright 1955, 1957 by Jack Kerouac. Reprinted by permission of Viking Penguin Inc.

Denver. Josiah M. Fleming, general manager of Daniels and Fisher Stores Company, built this Greek revival house in 1893. It was unusually simple compared to many of its overblown neighbors. *Sandra Dallas*

LaJunta. Another classic revival, this house was built in 1899 and is the grandest house in town. *Sandra Dallas*

Denver. The house is some kind of revival combination. The car and the driver are strictly early twentieth-century. *Courtesy Denver Public Library Western History Department.*

Pueblo. By the 1920s, many of Colorado's elegant Victorian homes had been converted to rooming houses. *Courtesy Pueblo Library District.*

6. Front Range Castles

THEY WERE AN AWESOME LOT, those nouveaux riches robber barons who carved fortunes out of the Colorado mountains and plains. They attacked life with the same ferocity they expended on their mining and industrial empires. They lived splendidly, lavishing fortunes on travel to Europe, medieval paintings, gaudy antiques, and useless ormolu-encrusted furniture. They sent their daughters to overpriced finishing schools and set up their sons in business. They transformed their wives into ladies and fancied themselves gentlemen. Most of all, they spent with

Denver. Real estate promoter and financier Donald Fletcher built his Grant Street mansion shortly before the 1893 silver crash, and during the depression that followed the drop in silver prices, he and his family lived in one corner of the unfinished house. Eventually the house was completed and had a skating rink and an art gallery. All that remains is the addition at the left, now owned by the Knights of Columbus. *Courtesy Denver Public Library Western History Department.*

Denver. Although sated with nouveau castles, Denverites nonetheless were agog at the William Church castle with its secret panels and pipe organ, its Norman tower and conservatory, and its staff of liveried servants. When Church, a copper and cattle magnate, died suddenly, his son closed the house, and rumors persisted that the ghost of William Church wandered the halls. Probably the ghosts were bootleggers. (No longer existent) *Courtesy Denver Public Library Western History Department.*

Denver. Onetime Denver & Rio Grande Western Railway Company surveyor J. A. McMurtrie built this grand palace. It was later acquired by John Good, whose brewery became the Tivoli-Union Brewing Company. (No longer existent) *Courtesy Denver Public Library Western History Department.*

Denver. Architect William Lang combined a hodgepodge of styles into this whimsical house for real-estate magnate Charles Kittredge. (No longer existent) *Courtesy Denver Public Library Western History Department.*

Denver. This chateau was built by Thomas B. Croke, who was uncomfortable living in the lavish house. He sold it to Thomas Patterson, publisher of the *Rocky Mountain News*. Patterson had no such qualms and lived in the house for years. Later converted to apartments and eventually offices, the Croke-Patterson House is home to at least one malevolent ghost. *Sandra Dallas*

Denver. Built of Longmont sandstone, the George W. Bailey mansion cost $45,000 to construct. Bailey, who made his fortune in real estate and trolleys, decorated the inside with every conceivable kind of wood—butternut in the library, black ash in the study, white mahogany and bird's-eye maple in the bedrooms, and even Texas pine and black ash in the servants' quarters. For many years the house was a restaurant, the Tiffin. *Sandra Dallas*

Manitou Springs. Briarhurst was built in 1888 for Dr. William Abraham Bell, one of the English socialites who caused Colorado Springs to be dubbed "Little London." Designed in Gothic revival style, Briarhurst, named for Bell's first Manitou home which burned, was described by a travel writer as "a typical English home . . . with rambling porches and picturesque gables." There was a fireplace in every room and an orchard, a greenhouse, and a tennis court on the 20-acre estate. *Sandra Dallas*

Denver. Jeffrey Keating, lumberman and real estate investor, paid the munificent sum of $18,000 to build this Romanesque revival house about 1892. *Sandra Dallas*

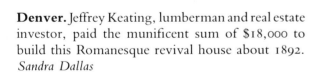

Manitou Springs. Cripple Creek saloonkeeper John Nolan, who liked to style himself "Honest John Nolan," bought this hillside house in 1900, a decade after it was built. In addition to his Cripple Creek watering spots, Nolan owned two Manitou Springs saloons, one of them with silver dollars embedded in its floor. *Sandra Dallas*

abandon on enormous homes that proclaimed to the world their extraordinary success.

On the Front Range prairie that was only a generation away from log cabins and sod huts, they created stone castles encrusted with Tiffany stained glass, hand-carved woodwork, gold- and silver-plated light fixtures, and splendid ballrooms. They erected crenelated palaces of outsize rusticated stone, indented with porches, pierced with battlements, with soaring towers capped by spikes that pierced the sky. The castles were surrounded by a collection of smaller replicas that served as garden cottages and carriage houses and various other outbuildings.

There were scores of these mostly self-made big spenders in Colorado in the 1880s and early 1890s. Before the 1893 silver crash, Denver, in fact, had "the largest army of landed millionaires to be found west of the Mississippi river," newspaper editor Frank Hall claimed. Never mind that the other major cities of the mountain West were Santa Fe, which was still a dingy mud-hut town, and Salt Lake City, where castles were built for God, not man. Still, by any yardstick, the Front Range cities of Denver, Colorado Springs, and Pueblo had an impressive number of newly minted tycoons setting up housekeeping in baronial splendor.

121

Denver. Silver magnate H. A. W. Tabor purchased this house for his beloved second wife, Baby Doe. The Tabors and their daughters, Lillie and Rose Mary Echo Silver Dollar, lived here until Tabor lost his fortune in the silver crash. At one time peacocks roamed the yard, and Baby Doe drove about in a carriage with a driver whose livery matched the color of her eyes. (No longer existent) *Author's Collection*.

Baby Doe, who scandalized the neighbors because she was a divorcee, further shocked them by putting statues of nudes on the lawn, but the interior was conventional Victorian. *Courtesy Colorado Historical Society.*

Pueblo. Thirty years after he arrived in Pueblo in a wagon filled with merchandise for sale, John A. Thatcher moved into Rosemount, completed in 1893 at a cost of nearly $100,000. Merchant and banker Thatcher demanded the finest—gas and electric lights, frescoes, elaborately carved woodwork, Tiffany chandeliers, ten fireplaces, and a copper-lined water tank that provided the house with 1,500 gallons of water. The house was called Rosemount after Mrs. Thatcher's favorite flower, and there were roses everywhere, from the parlor ceiling to the silver and china in the dining room. No one but Thatchers ever occupied the house. (Now a museum) *Sandra Dallas*

Denver. Elizabeth Sarah Frazier, who came west to sell sewing machines, married wealthy Colorado cattleman John W. Iliff in 1870. Only a few years after they married, Iliff died, leaving his widow one of the wealthiest women in Colorado. After she married Bishop Henry Warren, Lizzie funded the University of Denver's theology school and built Fitzroy Place, named for her hometown in Canada. It is a tossup whether the seminary or the house is larger. Both are built of massive stone blocks. After seventy-five years of Iliff-Warren ownership, Mrs. Warren's daughter left the house to the Theology School in 1966. Today it is a private school. *Sandra Dallas*

Colorado Springs. General William Jackson Palmer "wanted a castle, and above all, an old castle. And, as Colorado is peculiarly free of old castles, he had to build one for himself," wrote Julian Street. This was but a small problem for the immensely wealthy Palmer, founder of the Denver & Rio Grande. Glen Eyrie had an oak-paneled baronial hall, a bell to call guests from all over the estate for meals, roof tiles from an English church, and twenty-four fireplaces, though there are no chimneys. Instead, the smoke is conducted through a tunnel and emitted out of sight of the house. *Sandra Dallas*

Pueblo. Four generations of the Gast family lived in this mansion with its basement bowling alley and secret panels, built by Charles Edwin Gast in 1892. The first Gast was an attorney and city father who had a law partnership with U.S. Senator Alva B. Adams and counted Pueblo's wealthy Thatcher family among his clients. *Sandra Dallas*

Denver. No surface was left unadorned in this now demolished mansion. *Courtesy Colorado Historical Society.*

The state's biggest building boom, until the profligate oil-rich days of the 1970s, came in the six-year period that ended in 1893. In Denver alone, the construction included the $1.5 million Brown Palace Hotel and the $1.5 million Equitable Building, along with the Masonic Temple, the Post Office Building, the Boston Building, and the Kittredge Building. Men who built such edifices to commerce were just as eager to flaunt their wealth in personal statements of glory. The same architects who designed the commercial edifices were called upon to build mansions, men such as Frank E. Edbrooke, architect of the Brown Palace, and William Lang, who designed Saint Mark's Episcopal Church. Those architects loved the challenge of building the most impressive structures that ever appeared in Colorado.

They eschewed the lesser designs that had gone before. "The latter half of the nineteenth century produced . . . the ugliest architecture in the world . . . the square, squatty villas with their cupolas . . . and the stiff, narrow-gabled white frame buildings," wrote twentieth-century architect Lester Varian in a eulogy to his architect father, Ernest Philip Varian. The father and his partner,

127

Denver. Scotsman John Mouat, who later lost his lumber and loan company fortunes in the 1893 silver panic, built this handsome mansion in Denver's Highlands area. Subdivided into apartments, it was the scene of two gruesome murders in the 1970s. *Sandra Dallas*

Pueblo. This forty-room sandstone mansion, built at a cost of some $60,000 in 1890, was purchased by James Orman for $7,500 at a bankruptcy sale. When Orman was elected governor, he moved to the Molly Brown House in Denver. In 1917 the Pueblo mansion was purchased by another Colorado governor, Alva Adams. It remained in the Adams family until the 1950s. *Sandra Dallas*

Denver. Baron Walter von Richthofen, a relative of the famed Red Baron, built Richthofen Castle as an example of the house he wanted in his ambitious Denver subdivision, Montclair. The subdivision and health resort failed to prosper. In 1898 von Richthofen died and his body was returned to his native Germany. *Courtesy Denver Public Library Western History Department.*

Denver. William Garrett Fisher got rich furnishing the mansions of other
Colorado elite. A partner in the posh Daniels and Fisher Stores Company,
Fisher built this neoclassical revival mansion after the silver crash, which
may explain its restrained appearance. Or maybe it was good taste. Fisher's
wife later spent $75,000 adding the art gallery, *left. Sandra Dallas*

Denver. When he settled down to enjoy his money, farm boy turned cattle king turned merchant prince Dennis Sheedy built this mansion on Grant Street, dubbed "Gold Street" for its millionaire residents. Later, under the ownership of Helen Bonfils, it housed music studios, and following her death, the house was one of Denver's first elegant office mansions. *Sandra Dallas*

Littleton. Politico and bon vivant U.S. Senator Edward Oliver Wolcott threw a fashionable party for Denver society when he opened his rustic twelve-room summer cottage on the South Platte River in 1891. A few years later he turned it into this palatial Tudor retreat where he entertained Theodore Roosevelt. In 1901 he christened an expanded Wolhurst, as the house was named, with a three-day stag party and drunk. Later owners included Thomas F. Walsh, discoverer of the rich Camp Bird Mine, who entertained President William Howard Taft at a Wolhurst breakfast, and Horace Wilson Bennett, who made a killing in Cripple Creek real estate. (No longer existent) *Courtesy Denver Public Library Western History Department.*

Varian wrote, "loved the grandeur of the romanesque and with the sensibility of good artists they used the pink Manitou sandstone, and terra cotta, in those buildings which are today so graceful." With the aid of land developers and the magnates themselves, the elder Varian and other architects set about to enthrone the empire builders in suitable castles.

In Denver, Henry C. Brown, whose Brown Palace has been the height of luxury for nearly a century, turned a tract of prairie into the state's most snobbish subdivision, Capitol Hill. The wealthy snapped up lots with unbecoming haste. Colorado Springs millionaires erected their mansions not far from the Garden of the Gods or nestled them into the mountainsides. Pueblo tycoons built above their sprawling town in wealthy enclaves. Some people considered it odd to see the new castles looming on the treeless brown plains. "Such houses may be set in rolling country with good effect, but in the face of the vast mountain range . . . the most elaborate architecture is so completely

133

Denver. Among the last of the empire builders, David H. Moffat lived only briefly in his splendid dream house, and legend says he never even ate a meal in the lavish dining room. Pressed by failing business investments, Moffat, who nearly ruined the First National Bank of Denver through his poor management, was in New York attempting to raise money for another dream, a tunnel through the Rocky Mountains, when he died suddenly. He left two legacies that came to fruition long after his death. In 1928 the Moffat Tunnel was opened. In 1973 the fight to save the Moffat mansion was lost, but it led to Denver's strong historic preservation movement. *Courtesy Denver Public Library Western History Department.*

The Tiffany window in the Moffat mansion was reported to have cost $25,000. *Courtesy Denver Public Library Western History Department.*

Denver. James J. Brown paid $30,000 for this mansion on Quality Hill in 1894, and his wife, Margaret Tobin Brown, used it as a base to launch an assault on Denver society. Not until she emerged as the heroine of the *Titanic* disaster, however, was the "Unsinkable Molly Brown" (she acquired the name Molly in a 1960s musical) accepted by Denver's elite. (Now a museum) *Sandra Dallas*

Before one of her extravagant parties, which Denver society pointedly ignored, Maggie Brown hired a photographer to record her house, to the delight of the museum's curators. The entrance hall is encrusted with gilt and staffed by plaster Nubian slaves. *Courtesy Denver Public Library Western History Department.*

A slave to fashion and pretense, Maggie Brown furnished her house with the latest books, though it is doubtful if she read them. *Courtesy Denver Public Library Western History Department.*

137

Denver. The Browns also entertained at their 240-acre chicken farm at the edge of Denver. Maggie named it "Avoca" after a poem. *Sandra Dallas*

Idaho Springs. One did not have to be rich, merely imaginative, to have a stone castle. *Courtesy Denver Public Library Western History Department.*

Pueblo. While large size was desirable, some smaller houses were elaborate enough to be classified as castles. An architect–contractor team developed Pitkin Place as an exclusive block-long subdivision. Several executives of Colorado Fuel and Iron Company lived in the houses. *Sandra Dallas*

Denver. This impish house watched over by mythical creatures in the stonework was built for Adolph J. Zang, a brewer. *Sandra Dallas*

dwarfed as to seem almost ridiculous," noted Julian Street, the peripetetic magazine writer, who incensed some Coloradans with his unflattering observations. "Architecture cannot compete with the Rocky Mountains."

Colorado empire builders paid him no heed. They happily ripped up the Rocky Mountains to build their homes. Not only did they select homesites on the mountainsides, they gouged the granite and sandstone out of the earth to make building blocks for their castles.

For a decade or so these magnificent palaces thrust their way into the Colorado sky, stone by carefully rusticated stone, monuments to the men who guided the state's destiny. It was a period of wealth unknown in Colorado before or since. Not only were the mountain barons rich and powerful, they were empire builders, carving a state out of mountain and plain. They built personal empires from mining and agriculture and real estate, and they also platted cities and criss-crossed the state with railroads. Their decisions directed the state for seventy-five years. Their wives set

141

Fort Collins. Surveyor Franklin C. Avery went west with Nathan Meeker to form a colony at Greeley. After laying out that town, he platted Fort Collins and stayed to build this fairytale cottage in 1879. Among his family was his mother-in-law, who had reluctantly come west and who thereafter spent her days watching the trains depart for the East. Now a museum. *Sandra Dallas*

Denver. This elaborate series of houses was an attempt to bring row houses to Denver. They were never very popular. (Only partly existent) *Sandra Dallas*

Denver. Like a lonely sentinel, the 1888 Curry-Chucovich house is all that is left of a once prosperous downtown Denver neighborhood. James M. Curry used stone from his own quarries for the foundation of his house. In 1902, Vasco L. Chucovich, gambling linchpin, acquired the house. *Sandra Dallas*

Colorado's social and humanistic goals by establishing hospitals and churches and organizing charitable institutions. They also dictated social and moral standards.

For the wealthy, opulence was the norm. There were battalions of liveried servants the likes of which were unknown between Chicago and San Francisco. Lavish dinners were served on gold and silver plates set on massive carved tables. Then the gentlemen retired to talk politics over port and cigars, and the ladies gossiped and sipped coffee from paper-thin china demitasse cups in gilded salons. There was never a time in Colorado of such heavy spending, of such sanctimonious wealth.

Then came the silver crash, and the time for building castles on the prairie was over. While many of the western robber barons still carried on with abandon, there were few new ones to immor-

Denver. On occasion, the craftsmen who labored on Colorado's grand palaces enjoyed their own work. Stonemen's Row, made up of eight dwellings, was home to local stone workers. *Sandra Dallas*

talize themselves with stone palaces. Many of the empire builders were down and out. Silver king H. A. W. Tabor was so poor he had to carry water from the courthouse well to his Capitol Hill mansion. And not long afterward, William Lang, who had gotten rich from architectural commissions, moved from an elegant townhouse to a rooming house and, like his outdated stone castles, died impoverished, under mysterious circumstances.

145

7. White Boxes on the Prairie

NOT EVERYONE came looking for gold. The gaunt men and the sunburned, sun-bonneted women who settled the prairie also were searching for a better way of life. They found it, not in a hole in the ground that gave up riches, but in land.

From the swamplands of the Mississippi River, from the lush lands of the Old South, now scorched and bloodied by an appalling Civil War, from the rocky, worn farms of New England, these searchers loaded their goods into lumbering wagons, climbed aboard, and headed for the desolate plains of eastern Colorado. They were farmers, or hoped to be, and they had been lured for more than half a century by the promise of cheap Colorado land.

The women were frightened, their eyes restlessly searching the plains for a sign of gentleness, hoping for a stream, a tree, or some small reassurance of civilization. The men were silent, hopeful, as

Buckingham. Eastern Colorado's domestic architecture was a simple, no-frills style. Hundreds of deserted boxes, once painted white and home to forgotten families, dot the eastern plains of Colorado. *Sandra Dallas*

Kim. Composition siding once covered this house in what probably was a futile attempt to keep out the winter cold. *Sandra Dallas*

Severance. Isolated one- or two-room buildings still house families. The basement probably is warmer in winter than the first floor. *Sandra Dallas*

147

Springfield. The south-facing porch, covered with vines, gave shade in the summer. *Sandra Dallas*

East of **Ault.** The two doors indicate this white box may have been a duplex. *Sandra Dallas*

Boulder. Vines and tin cans of geraniums in the windows, along with the bird cages and tiny American flag, relieve the plainness of this simple house. *Courtesy Denver Public Library Western History Department.*

West of **Ordway.** Two added wings and a front porch indicate this farm was more prosperous than most. *Sandra Dallas*

Raymer. This variation of the white box has a clipped gable and a decorative gable window. *Sandra Dallas*

West of **Olney Springs.** This clipped-gable box is constructed of cast concrete blocks covered with stucco. *Sandra Dallas*

Ordway. In what was sheer abandon for the restrained eastern plains, this
house sports a front porch with turned posts and gingerbread brackets and a
decorative fan in the gable. *Sandra Dallas*

Brush. The eastern plains' ubiquitous house style is the "prairie box."
Sandra Dallas

Merino. There were a hundred variations of the prairie box. This one has a
small porch with a touch of gingerbread trim. People in eastern Colorado
still sit on the porch and watch the cars go by. *Sandra Dallas*

Flagler. Diminutive prairie boxes. *Sandra Dallas*

LaJunta. Although built of stone with accented quoins and a fanciful porch, this house is nonetheless prairie box in style. *Sandra Dallas*

153

West of **Bent's Old Fort.** The same style in adobe. *Sandra Dallas*

they clutched at the earth and smelled it as it sifted through their fingers.

They told each other they could build homes here on the plains, and they set out to slice the sod into building material and to plant crops. To their surprise, they found the land was kind; the earth was fertile, producing not only crops but trees and flowers to soften the landscape.

In time, the harshness subsided and a certain prosperity set in. But these people had been tempered by the spartan land. Unlike their contemporaries in the mountains, whose free-spending ways were prompted by easy money, the farmers on the eastern plains were little tempted to spend their money for ostentatious houses.

They abandoned the dirt houses, but rarely replaced them with more than frame replicas of those first-generation dwellings. They built small, square frame houses, most of them not trimmed with gingerbread, though often they sported practical porches. Invariably, the houses were painted white, like the churches and the schools. "Comfortable but unpretentious," historian Frank Hall called them. In summer the little white boxes defied the sun, while in winter they stood with their porches around them like

Salida. The closer to the mountains, the more elaborate the house. The elegant porch and cornice brackets almost obscure the house's box shape. *Kendal Atchison*

protective arms to keep out the cold. The houses were often over-shadowed by well-kept barns and accompanied by nondescript collections of shacks and outbuildings that were used for chicken coops or for storing everything from farm implements to dis-carded furniture to trunks of mementoes. Almost certainly there was a cellar for the harvest from a kitchen garden—bushel baskets of potatoes and onions, jars of home-canned peas and peaches and venison, cases of store-bought canned goods.

The most common of the little white houses was the "prairie box," a frame square with a pyramidal roof topped by a chimney, and often there was a front porch. The style could be enlarged with the addition of a lean-to at the side or back. Sometimes the lean-to was built of stone or brick.

The white frame houses were planted on solitary farms pro-tected by windbreaks of trees or along town streets lined with trees and lawns. Those unrelieved white boxes, as simple inside as out, became as distinctive on the eastern plains of Colorado as the fanciful gingerbread houses were in the mountains. Succeeding generations have built bigger houses on the plains, but they still are frame and angular and almost always painted white.

155

Boulder. The decorative porch and the landscaping make this square a stylish house. *Courtesy Denver Public Library Western History Department.*

Denver. A far cry from its country cousin, this prairie box in Curtis Park is
built of brick with carved stone lintels. *Sandra Dallas*

Genoa. The center section of this house probably was built first, with the
wings added as the family grew. *Sandra Dallas*

157

Southwest of **Greeley.** Mismatched siding on both the first and second stories indicates this house may have been a barn. *Kendal Atchison*

West of **Eaton.** Tiny saplings planted on the plains by early pioneers now provide relief from summer sun and winter wind. *Sandra Dallas*

Bennett. The wraparound porch gives protection from the elements but cannot hide the desolation of the Colorado plains. *Sandra Dallas*

South of **Julesburg.** Colorado's affluent early farmers built these sturdy two-story farmhouses with a variety of pasted-on porches and additions. *Sandra Dallas*

159

Sugar City. In contrast to their workers who lived in tiny cottages, officials of the National Sugar Manufacturing Company lived in fine houses, such as this one built for the company manager. On occasion, National's president stayed in the house with his wife, who took great interest in the town children and gave them cream-filled candy eggs at holidays. The house was built with a parlor, a library, a dining room, a kitchen, and three bedrooms, but only one bath. A laundry house was in back. *Courtesy Colorado Historical Society.*

The sugar factory shut down in 1967, and the house was abandoned. The front yard was once planted in alfalfa, but it was allowed to die out after water used to flood the crop ran into the basement of the manager's house. *Sandra Dallas*

8. Age of Elegance

COLORADO EMERGED from the 1893 silver depression with a sense of elegance, sophistication, and self-confidence it had never before shown. Turn-of-the-century sleekness and refinement replaced the big-spender image of the Front Range barons that had manifested itself in the ponderous castles that were quickly becoming anachronisms. "Like the ghost towns of the West which bespeak another and perhaps better day, are the ghost houses, mute evidence of another era, another trend in the mode of the lives of the rich," wrote a *Rocky Mountain News* society writer.

Perhaps as a reaction to the Gilded Age, there was a move to the simpler, more symmetrical neoclassical and revival styles. Even the commercial structures that went up after the turn of the century displayed grace and restraint, at least as compared to the for-

Denver. At the turn of the century, Colorado's elite wanted homes that denoted elegance and serenity, not the frenzy of empire building. *Courtesy Denver Public Library Western History Department.*

Denver. Former Colorado Governor James Benton Grant began construction of this splendid beaux arts mansion in 1900 and finished it two years later at a cost of only $35,000. In 1917 it was acquired by oil tycoon Albert E. Humphreys, who turned the bowling alley into a shooting gallery and added a ten-car garage. The mansion remained in the Humphreys family until 1976 when it was willed to the Colorado Historical Society. (Now a museum) *Sandra Dallas*

Denver. Begun in 1904 by Walter Scott Cheesman, who did not live to see it completed, this Georgian revival was occupied until 1923 by his daughter and her husband, John Evans. Later owners Mr. and Mrs. Claude K. Boettcher filled the house with antiques and replaced the awninged garden room with an elegant palm court, painted white because Mrs. Boettcher felt white enhanced her looks. Today it is the Colorado Governor's Mansion. *Courtesy Denver Public Library Western History Department.*

Denver. Frederick G. Bonfils, cofounder of the *Denver Post,* lived in this house until his death in 1933. Once, when threats were made on his life, a guard with a machine gun was stationed on the balcony above the front door. Inside there was silver leaf in the dining room ceiling, a carving of a child's head above a fireplace, and the tapestry on the walls was reported to cost $75 a yard. (No longer existent) *Courtesy Denver Public Library Western History Department.*

Denver. For years this house, built in 1906, was the home of William E. Sweet, who used it for official functions when he was governor. Sweet had a running feud with his next-door neighbor, Harry H. Tammen, cofounder of the *Denver Post. Courtesy Denver Public Library Western History Department.*

Denver. Great Western Sugar Company head William Lloyd Petrikin, known as "Squire" Petrikin, built this house in 1917. During World War II, volunteers were allowed on the roof to spot airplanes. *Sandra Dallas*

Denver. This Georgian revival is reported to be the first house in Denver built with steel beam construction. More apparent are the elegant leaded glass sliding doors between the living room and the dining room and a stained glass window depicting a scene from *Romeo and Juliet. Sandra Dallas*

Boulder. Retired lumberman John McInnes built this house for his young bride. McInnes took the design from a pattern book and selected a variety of rare woods for the interior. The McInnes children roller skated in the third-floor ballroom. *Sandra Dallas*

Denver. Brewery magnate Adolph Coors built this home on Denver's Cheesman Park for his daughter Augusta. The house incorporated carvings of children's heads in the ironwork balcony, in the stone arches above the doors, and in friezes under the windows. (No longer existent) *Courtesy Denver Public Library Western History Department.*

Denver. Fiery Lena Stoiber, known as "Captain Jack" in Silverton where one of her husbands made a fortune in mining, built this elegant house in 1907. For years Denverites gossiped that a subsequent husband, who had booked passage on the *Titanic,* actually missed the boat, but when the ship sank, he saw his chance and disappeared anyway. *Denver Public Library Western History Department.*

In later years Stoiberhof, as it was originally called, was owned by Mrs. Verner Z. Reed and then by Albert E. Humphreys, Jr., who grew up in the Grant-Humphreys Mansion. *Sandra Dallas*

Colorado Springs. Influenced by having lived among the ostentatious mansions of Newport, Charles Baldwin felt right at home in this 22,000-square-foot French palace. McKim, Mead, and White of New York City designed the house in 1904 after the Grand Trianon at Versailles. The Baldwins called the forty-room mansion Claremont, but later owners renamed it, more appropriately, Trianon. *Sandra Dallas*

171

Denver. As leader of the "Sacred 36" (so-called because thirty-six persons made up nine tables of bridge), Mrs. Crawford Hill ruled Denver society from this mansion. She scandalized old Denver society with her cocktail parties and tea dances. Today the house is the Town Club. *Courtesy Denver Public Library Western History Department.*

Crawford Hill's picture hangs from the balcony. The larger portrait is of Bulkeley Wells, manager of the Smuggler–Union Mine near Telluride and reputedly Mrs. Hill's lover. *Courtesy Denver Public Library Western History Department.*

Mrs. Hill's picture hangs in the dining room. *Courtesy Denver Public Library Western History Department.*

Denver. Helen Bonfils, daughter of *Denver Post* founder Frederick Bonfils, lived in this French Mediterranean home for many years. Built about 1910, the house, once owned by Phyllis McGuire, one of the singing McGuire Sisters, has been converted to condominiums. *Sandra Dallas*

A philanthropist and theater impresario, "Miss Helen" frequently entertained in the garden. *Courtesy Denver Public Library Western History Department.*

Denver. Oscar Malo, president of Colorado Milling and Elevator Company, built this Italian villa in 1921. In the library there is a secret panel that opens to reveal a prohibition-era liquor cabinet. *Sandra Dallas*

Colorado Springs. Spencer Penrose turned a tidy investment in Cripple Creek gold into a magnificent fortune by backing a process to treat low-grade copper ore. He was one of the West's legendary playboys and big spenders and built the Broadmoor resort in 1918. El Pomar, shown in 1920, near the Broadmoor, was home base for Penrose and his wife, Julie. *Courtesy Denver Public Library Western History Department.*

tified office buildings and civic structures of the nineteenth century. Houses followed suit. Although there still were plenty of rich Coloradans around, their homes were decidedly pared down when compared with the stone castles of the empire builders. The richest miner of them all was, perhaps, Spencer Penrose, who made a modest fortune in Cripple Creek gold and then parlayed it into a king's ransom by investing in copper. He eschewed the castlelike architecture of other Colorado Springs millionaires and selected instead a flowing villa with the deprecating name of "El Pomar"—The Apple Orchard. Others followed suit.

Like Penrose, Colorado's wealthy young citizens preferred stylish villas to stone mausoleums. Elizabethan chateaus (architectural purity was still unimportant) replaced crenelated Norman fortresses. The baronial look of the 1880s, in fact, was suspect, ungracious. One old-style Colorado castle, the Croke-Patterson mansion in Denver, was now described by the *News's* writer

The Penroses entertained lavishly in the garden of El Pomar and in the tea-house at the back. The estate is now owned by the Roman Catholic church. *Courtesy Denver Public Library Western History Department.*

as resembling "a turret towering on the sidewalk. It seems to threaten and frown on all that pass." (See photograph on page 118.)

The new mansions, in contrast, were more inviting. They had open floor plans and were spacious. Homebuilders discovered sunlight. Whereas the Victorian castle dwellers had carried out their duties in rooms darkened by walnut shutters and heavy velvet draperies to protect their complexions as well as their furniture, their descendants opened the windows and let the sunlight flood their homes.

Landscaping became important, too. In Denver, Mayor Robert W. Speer began a "city beautiful" movement and designed a series of parks and parkways to enhance the quality of the city's life. Homeowners followed suit. Gone were uninspired rose bowers and insipid kitchen gardens, in favor of flowing lawns with fountains and carefully kept flower beds.

Denver. When Mr. and Mrs. Richard Crawford Campbell moved into this house in 1927, their neighbor, Squire Petrikin, led a parade of bagpipers playing "The Campbells Are Coming" to greet them. The house has a secret staircase that connects the library, the master bedroom, and the wine cellar. *Sandra Dallas*

Designed by J. J. B. Benedict, known for his romantic touch, the house is now headquarters for the Denver Botanic Gardens Foundation. *Sandra Dallas*

Denver. Benedict also was architect of this stylish villa (*above*), which backs onto Cheesman Park, and this Seventh Avenue house (*below*). *Sandra Dallas*

179

Denver. This elegant French chateau, another Benedict design, was built overlooking the Denver Country Club and surrounded by formal gardens. In addition to parquet floors, Italian marble fireplaces, Italian plasterwork, and crystal chandeliers, the house has a campy art-deco ballroom and a theater in its basement. *Courtesy Denver Public Library Western History Department.*

Douglas County. In 1891, John W. Springer began construction of a ranch house he dubbed "Castle Isabel," for his scandalous wife, who later was involved in a sensational Brown Palace murder. The house was expanded and remodeled through the 1920s and 1930s by Frank E. Kistler, who used it as a base for the Arapahoe Hunt, in which pink-coated riders and their hounds hunted for coyote instead of fox. The property, acquired in the 1930s by Lawrence C. Phipps, Jr., was later called Highlands Ranch. *Sandra Dallas*

The "Venneford Ranch" sign is left over from the television filming. In *Centennial,* the Venneford was owned by English interests. *Sandra Dallas*

In the 1970s, scenes for the television mini-series *Centennial,* based on the James A. Michener novel, were filmed at Highlands Ranch. *Sandra Dallas*

181

Denver. Verner Z. Reed made a fortune in gold and oil. His wife (shown with her dog) helped spend it on magnificent houses, first Stoiberhof (see page 170) and later this English-style mansion. *Denver Public Library Western History Department.*

Mrs. Reed, who lived in England for many years and who copied her mansion after a British home, was enamored of English architecture. She gave the University of Denver its two handsomest buildings, Mary Reed Building and Margery Reed Hall, both designed in English style. *Sandra Dallas*

Englewood. An English-style rival to the Reed mansion is this turreted latter-day castle built in the then fledgling elite suburb of Cherry Hills. *Courtesy Colorado Historical Society*

At the same time, Coloradans moved away from the tight little enclaves of the rich, such as Capitol Hill in Denver. By 1900, a *Denver Times* reporter noted that Capitol Hill "no longer implies the social leverage of a few years ago, when you were either on it or not on it. . . . One can no longer tell just·who you are by where you live."

It was an age of elegance, and the houses were built in an extraordinary variety of styles. First came the beaux arts designs and the revivals and the villas. Following World War I, the Tudor, the Jacobean, the Mediterranean, the mission, and even arts and crafts on a grand scale took over.

The greatest change in the homes of the rich came about because of changes in their life-style, manifested in far more practical houses with streamlined kitchens and the elimination of stables and carriage houses.

There were fewer servants, partly because the servant class moved away from domestic service into better-paying jobs. Moreover, the manufacture of labor-saving devices, such as gas stoves that replaced wood-burning cookstoves and appliances such as vacuum cleaners, meant fewer jobs for domestics. Automobiles replaced carriages, eliminating grooms and stablehands in favor of a single chauffeur-mechanic, and he, in turn, gave way as the

Denver. Senator and Mrs. Lawrence C. Phipps built this fifty-four-room mansion during the Great Depression from a sense of noblesse oblige; they wanted to provide work for unemployed craftsmen. It also was a way of getting cheap labor. The 8½-acre estate also boasts an enormous tennis ouse. *Courtesy Denver Public Library Western History Department.*

Too large to be operated as a private home today, the house is owned by the University of Denver. *Sandra Dallas*

The garden at Belcaro, as the Phipps called their home. *Courtesy Colorado Historical Society.*

185

Colorado Springs. About 1920, Maria McKean Allen demolished the English-style mansion her former husband had built in 1910 and built this slightly smaller near-replica. Despite its size, she referred to it as a "cottage." Today, it is an Episcopal chapel. *Sandra Dallas*

wealthy, including the women, took to the wheel themselves. Simpler styles of clothing allowed women to button their own dresses, and no longer was the personal maid necessary. The elimination of ground-sweeping petticoats and abundant underclothing meant less need for a laundress.

Society itself became less rigid, and that change was reflected in the domestic architecture. Gone were the surfeiting formal dinners with a footman standing behind each place to serve as a private waiter. Men and women mingled in society more freely. Gentlemen no longer retired to the library after dinner, but remained with the ladies. Cocktail parties replaced suffocating receptions; informal dances usurped formal balls. As time went on, the wealthy required fewer and fewer services. By the late thirties, many made do with a single maid and perhaps a cook, and madam herself sometimes did the cooking.

Not everyone got carried away with doing for oneself, of course. For some, a full contingent of servants remained indispensable. When Ruth Boettcher Humphreys, who lived in Lena Stoiber's magnificent house in Denver, died in 1959, she had in her employ

Denver (*above*); **Colorado Springs** (*below*). In the period between the two world wars, Tudor and Jacobean styles were popular among Colorado's well-to-do. *Sandra Dallas*

Englewood. Architects William E. and Arthur A. Fisher designed this home, built in 1920 for merchant prince George Gano and his wife Ethel, after an English hunt-country manor house. After Gano's death in 1929, his financially pressed widow sold the house to Hubert Work, a political power in the Harding and Coolidge administrations. Ethel Gano later married Work, who returned the house to her as a wedding present, and she swore she would never leave it. As she lay in state after her death in 1960 before the living room fireplace, a great beam in the ceiling cracked. Subsequent owners believe her benevolent presence remains in the house. *Courtesy Colorado Historical Society.*

Denver. Along with building new style houses, Denverites moved into fashionable new suburbs such as Country Club (*above*) and Morgan's Addition (*below*). *Courtesy Colorado Historical Society.*

189

Evergreen. The Gates family, who made a fortune in Gates Rubber Company, spent their summers at this mountain retreat. Like other mountain estates near Evergreen, Chateau Gates maintained a carefully manicured lawn.
Sandra Dallas

a dozen or so servants. A few other doyens of the old era held out almost as long, maintaining till death the standards of a bygone era. One Denver matron continued to hold court like "some Dresden empress in this castle-like, three-storied and many-roomed mansion," wrote the *News* reporter. But, she added, "Time marches on."

Indeed, it did. Colorado's period of refinement in domestic architecture ended with World War II. Although many of the mansions built during that era remain private homes today, they were not to be duplicated after the war. Economics, a more hectic lifestyle, and something called modern architecture combined to doom Colorado's age of elegance.

Denver. The whimsey of the Charles Boettcher II house, built in the 1920s for some $250,000, belied the tragedy that took place there. In 1933, Boettcher was kidnapped while parking his car in the garage. After two weeks he was ransomed. A few years later Boettcher's wife, Anna Lou Boettcher, shot herself and died in the master bedroom. (No longer existent) *Courtesy Denver Public Library Western History Department.*

9. Homes for All

As the state of Colorado matured, it became middle-class. After one last fling in Cripple Creek, the strike-it-rich spirit that made instant millionaires of impoverished prospectors disappeared. By the turn of the century, it was nearly impossible to become a millionaire by sheer luck.

But if the Colorado economy now limited the number of its magnates, it also limited the number of poverty-stricken people whose plight had been the dirty side of the early robber-baron society. Colorado moved to center stage, became egalitarian, and became largely populated by a staid, home-owning middle class.

Comfortable merchant and professional families with a servant or two settled on tree-lined streets. In the same neighborhood, fac-

Loveland. By the turn of the century, a comfortable house on a tree-lined street was the goal of most Coloradans. *Courtesy Denver Public Library Western History Department.*

Sopris. Coal–company towns with their look–alike houses were a precursor of tract housing. *Courtesy Colorado Historical Society.*

Rouse. Despite the cramped, unimaginative houses and the absence of lawns, which forced children to play in the dirt, company towns offered accommodations that were superior to the housing that immigrant coal miners had left behind in the old country. *Courtesy Colorado Historical Society.*

193

Trinidad. This prosperous middle-class house owned by photographer O. E. Aultman is a marriage between sensible cottage and late Victorian showiness. *Courtesy Colorado Historical Society.*

Part of the growing middle-class ethic was the enjoyment of leisure time, time to grow columbine or indulge in hobbies, such as photography. *Courtesy Colorado Historical Society.*

By the turn of the century, iron beds and serpentine-front dressers had replaced heavy Victorian walnut furniture. *Courtesy Colorado Historical Society.*

In 1905 the lady of the house could while away her free hours in her own Turkish corner or "cozy corner." *Courtesy Colorado Historical Society.*

195

South of **Nathrop.** Only the most successful farmers and ranchers could afford a rambling, red-brick bungalow like this one. In keeping with the farm ethic, however, the main entrance to this house is the back door. *Sandra Dallas*

Denver. Block after block of these stolid brick bungalows with their comfortable porches can be seen in any Colorado city. *Sandra Dallas*

Burlington. A fancier city version of a prairie box. *Sandra Dallas*

Denver. The sewing machine was a common labor-saving device that graced almost every early twentieth-century middle-class home. *Courtesy Denver Public Library Western History Department.*

Gunnison (*above*); **Grand Junction** (*below*). The arts-and-crafts bungalow
with half-timbering was at home in big city or small town. *Sandra Dallas*

199

Durango. The arts-and-crafts movement advocated the use of brick and stone. The bungalow, its fireplace, and even its garage are built of rounded river rocks.

Denver. Inside, the arts-and-crafts house often featured beamed ceilings, stained glass, and golden oak woodwork. This home was fashionably adorned with a golden oak library table and art pottery. *Courtesy Denver Public Library Western History Department.*

Denver. Golden oak was popular in the dining room too, in pre–Prohibition Colorado. *Courtesy Denver Public Library Western History Department.*

tory workers and clerks and bank tellers happily bought smaller homes. Whether large or small, the homes were equally well kept, with linoleum floors waxed to a shine and starched antimacassars pinned to the arms of overstuffed furniture. Trim green lawns abounded with clipped bushes and orderly flower beds.

Houses became important to a whole new class of people who had never before owned property. There were homes for all. In 1908 a Denver homebuilder asked in an advertisement:

> What comforts has a renter compared with the man who owns his own home? Home comforts and independence and the increase in property value should be yours. It is rightly yours and can be yours if you put your foot down and say, you will stop paying rent.
>
> We are offering every man an opportunity to own a home of his own at a price he can afford to pay and practically upon his own terms. Will you come around and see us about it or will you continue to make some persons still richer off your labors?

Denver. With Prohibition in effect and the saloon stop after work a thing of the past, many working men channeled their energy into such constructive projects as yard work, though few achieved the perfection of this prize-winning yard with rock garden, pergola, and lily pond. *Courtesy Denver Public Library Western History Department.*

What aspiring homeowner could resist such blandishments? Few did. To meet the growing demand for houses for the middle class, Colorado builders turned to mass production. It was not the acres of tract houses that dropped on the prairies like hailstones following World War II, merely half a dozen look-alikes along a single block. A good middle-class house could be purchased for well under $10,000. A do-it-yourselfer or one willing to oversee the construction work could buy a kit for a two-story frame house with a porch and a bay window from the 1918 Sears, Roebuck & Company catalog for only $1,465.

Hometown newspapers vied with each other in touting the number of homes built each year. In June 1901, for example, the *Denver Times* noted that residential building permits totaling $1.1 million had been issued for houses in the first six months of the year. The most popular section of the city was Capitol Hill, with 105 residences costing an average of $4,860.

Although price was important, quality mattered too. Homeowners wanted solid brick houses with insulation and central heat and nickel plumbing. They wanted houses that said "solid and secure and moving up." "A very desirable feature in purchasing a

Inside and out, Gwenthean Cottage, located in Chautauqua Park, was a model of good design and healthful living. Ammons frequently gave lectures on her cottage. *Courtesy Anne McLaughlin Long.*

Boulder. Gwenthean Cottage was designed and built as a model cottage about 1900 by Theodosia G. Ammons, who was head of the Department of Domestic Science at Colorado State University. *Courtesy Anne McLaughlin Long.*

home . . . is that your house is new and modern and is situated among houses of the same class," wrote a Colorado builder who constructed red-brick bungalows.

This forty-year period of middle-class homebuilding led to several popular styles. One was the bungalow, originally named for the tidy cottages that housed English workers in India. The smug little bungalow, with its serviceable front porch, was popular because it was comfortable and could be dressed up in a hundred different ways. The Tudor cottage, which followed the bungalow, was more expensive and had an element of sophistication. And then there was the foursquare, that sturdy brick rectangle with its sensible arrangement of rooms that was so popular in Denver that it was dubbed the "Denver square."

For builders of middle-class houses, the watchword was simplicity. "Only in such simplicity and sincerity can a nation develop a condition of permanent and properly equalized welfare," wrote Gustav Stickley, a proponent of the craftsman style of archi-

MAY YOUR RECENT ACQUISITION
INCREASE YOUR JOY AND PROSPERITY
THIS CHRISTMAS

VAN SCHAACK & CO.

Denver. This bungalow was the epitome of the arts-and-crafts movement—beamed ceilings, bare wood floors, and plain brick fireplace. Compared to the Victorian interiors it replaced, the decor was simplicity itself. *Courtesy Colorado Historical Society.*

Denver. In 1945 the purchase of a bungalow like this, with music room, enclosed sunporch, and finished basement, was a step up for almost anybody. To remind them of their good fortune, the real estate agent sent a Christmas card with a picture of the recently purchased house. *Courtesy Harriett Dallas.*

Delta. Like the gingerbread cottages they replaced, bungalows had personality. *Sandra Dallas*

Mesita. This abandoned cottage was built from local stone. *Kendal Atchison*

Trinidad. Bungalows were supposed to be one story, but the style could be expanded comfortably into two. *Sandra Dallas*

Antonito. The Frank Warshauer house is a bungalow design gone riot. The mansion, whose wings resemble two overblown bungalows, was elegantly decorated inside with painted friezes depicting the world's great thinkers and politicians. The block-square estate once included a tennis court. *Sandra Dallas*

Denver. In the 1930s, Tudor cottages began replacing the less sophisticated bungalows. *Sandra Dallas*

Denver. Like bungalows, these small Tudors offered economy of space but with more elegance and class. *Sandra Dallas*

Pueblo. As the family automobile became more common, hundreds of these fashionable bungalows and cottages were built in suburban settings. *Courtesy Pueblo Library District.*

tecture, which advocated simple, unpainted wood, the elimination of useless ornamentation, and economy of space.

Stickley also encouraged simple, unadorned decors with a minimum of clutter, which would eliminate unnecessary housework. Antimacassars required wool or cotton thread, which required knitting or crochet needles and a box in which to store them, then a table for the box, and so on, Stickley wrote. That kind of clutter raised "such a dust of trivialities," he wrote in his book *Craftsman Homes,* "that if a chariot of fire were sent to fetch us, ten to one we should not see it." Chariots of fire aside, Stickley's ideas on decor were generally ignored, and housewives who appreciated Stickley's other labor-saving designs happily cluttered their homes with doilies to protect their furniture and dust-collecting bric-a-brac.

The homes-for-all period was Colorado's time for settling in. Thousands of bungalows and cottages and squares were built in virtually every Colorado town and city. It urbanized Colorado and still represents the domestic heart of many communities. Unlike the castles and the gingerbread cottages, the foursquares and the Tudors and the bungalows rarely became rooming houses and office buildings. In fact, many of the middle-class neighborhoods built between the silver crash and the beginning of World War II

Denver. Gaming kingpin Ed Chase, who controlled Denver gambling from the town's founding well into the twentieth century, lived in this Curtis Park Italianate house, a forerunner of the Denver square. (No longer existent) *Courtesy Denver Public Library Western History Department.*

Denver. Another foursquare transitional was this downtown townhouse. (No longer existent) *Sandra Dallas*

213

Denver. To Colorado's growing middle class, a Denver square on a bucolic tree-lined street was the American dream house. *Author's Collection.*

Denver. The ubiquitous Denver square could be dressed in various porches and window designs, but it still was a Denver square. *Sandra Dallas*

have changed little from the early twentieth century when historian Jerome C. Smiley wrote that Denver

is a city of many beautiful homes . . . impressive to the stranger, and potent incentives to the citizen who sees them every day. There are hundreds that exhibit striking, tasteful, harmonious designs. . . . Residences are not crowded together; they do not shoulder each other but are surrounded by lawns set with shrubbery and flowers. . . . In all that men have done in the upbuilding of this city, the beautiful homes they have erected constitute the glory of their work.

Denver. Almost without exception, the square had a living room, a dining room, a kitchen and a pantry, and an entrance hall on the first floor, with three bedrooms and a bath on the second. *Courtesy Denver Public Library Western History Department.*

Denver. This better-than-average Denver square housed a better-than-average Denver family—the Douds, whose daughter, Mamie (shown standing between two servants and holding her pet rabbit) would marry Dwight Eisenhower. *Courtesy Denver Public Library Western History Department.*

South of **Buena Vista.** Not all Denver squares were in Denver. This square is a mountain meadow ranch house. *Sandra Dallas*

10. Colorado Moderne

Though Colorado embraced most of the housing styles that came rolling across the prairie from the East, the state had only a brief flirtation with the modern styles that surfaced in the 1920s and 1930s. Art deco was popular for the most part in commercial structures such as Denver's Mayan Theater, where reliefs of grotesque Aztec figures and shiny glazed tile seemed appropriate to the Hollywood extravaganzas that played there. Another was the Kress store in Pueblo, where the gaudy tilework

Denver. A prelude to the age of "modern" architecture was this art-deco fantasy with its Moroccan touches. The upper story and the solar collector are late additions. *Sandra Dallas*

Pueblo. The whitewashed look of mission-style architecture, with its scallops and decorative windows, was another moderne precursor. *Sandra Dallas*

Denver. This elegant mission villa was built with a second-floor ballroom.
Sandra Dallas

Denver. While not an art-deco house, this Denver home nonetheless has many of the decorative arts touches that made art deco appealing. *Courtesy Denver Public Library Western History Department.*

Denver. The most famous of all Colorado moderne houses is Shangri-la, built by Harry Huffman, local theater mogul. Huffman first saw the house, the apogee of 1930s Hollywood glitz, in the movie *Lost Horizon* and had a local architect draw up the plans. *Sandra Dallas*

Denver. This unlandscaped modern house is a stark contrast to its more conventional neighbors. *Courtesy Denver Public Library Western History Department.*

reflected the glittering dime-store treasures within. The other modern styles—moderne and international—were only briefly popular, but they left behind a few, now quaint, examples that are still sought after because of the current interest in deco.

Moderne and international and deco—the names are used interchangeably if inaccurately in Colorado—are instantly recognizable. They were a tribute to technology, to new materials, to the glories of the machine age. They were part of a trend that glorified the modern era of sophisticated travel—sleek streamliner trains, fast motor cars, powerful airplanes. It was an age that worshipped men who dammed rivers and decimated forests, who saw the future in enormous factories filled with glistening machinery and efficient assembly lines. Moderne also could be a "funky" style, whimsical and theatrical.

No wonder that the architects who came of age in this era turned their skills to designing houses that reflected the modern materials and utilitarianism they saw elsewhere. Moderne was the ultimate rejection of fussy Victorian architecture.

For all its high ideals, moderne in Colorado had a touch of the tawdry, a sense of sensationalism. And little wonder; the two most famous examples of moderne housing in Denver (where most of these houses were built in Colorado) were connected with the theater. Shangri-la, a grand white mansion that stands imperiously

Denver. The neatly trimmed spherical tree is in keeping with the uncluttered lines of the house. *Sandra Dallas*

Pueblo (*top*); **Durango** (*center*); **Pueblo** (*bottom*). Moderne vernacular.
Sandra Dallas

Denver. This elegant little house was built as a home and studio by artist
Allen True. *Sandra Dallas*

Denver. Glass block and glazed tile were used by modern architects because of their contemporary look and easy-care properties. *Sandra Dallas*

Denver. Contemporary architects were intrigued with modern transportation designs and embellished their houses with the curved lines of a diesel locomotive, or the railings of a luxury liner, or the "speed" lines (rendered in black glass) that decorated automobiles. *Sandra Dallas*

229

Denver. In the mid-1930s, Harry Huffman gave away this highly publicized "Cinderella House," a sort of modern Georgian adaptation, to a lucky Fox Theater ticket buyer. An unmarried couple from out of town purchased the winning ticket and promptly sold the house. The architect and other professionals who worked on the house were expected to donate their services in exchange for publicity. *Courtesy Denver Public Library Western History Department.*

on a hill with a sweeping view of the doughnut shops and service stations of Colorado Boulevard, was built by Harry Huffman, head of Denver's Fox Inter-mountain Theaters, Incorporated. It was copied straight out of the 1933 motion picture *Lost Horizon*. And the "Cinderella House," another Huffman offering, was given away as part of a theater promotion.

Another strike against the style was that it was particularly unsuited for Colorado. Flat roofs were not designed for heavy snow loads, and the lack of roof overhangs to keep out the sun meant Colorado's bright sunlight faded furniture and rotted draperies. Even glass block, a mainstay of moderne, trapped the sun's heat so well that it overheated rooms. Moderne was the shortest lived of the housing styles. It ended with World War II, and though a few stripped-down houses emerged in the late 1940s, returning GIs had had too much contact with technology during the war. They

Denver. "Cinderella House" architect Paul Atchison adapted the same design for several east Denver houses. The decorative panel between the first and second story windows is copper. *Sandra Dallas*

wanted houses that said *home,* not stripped-down, glass-and-metal cages with prow fronts and decorative speed lines that reminded them more of troop carriers and bombers. A few examples of Colorado moderne remain, but many have been adulterated by aluminum and Plexiglas awnings to keep out the sun, as well as by wood siding added in a vain attempt to disguise an embarrassing flirtation with modern design.

231

Colorado Springs. The international style was even more stripped down than moderne. *Sandra Dallas*

Pueblo (*top*); **Denver** (*below*). The moderne style offered little protection from Colorado's bright sun, which is why awnings have been added. *Sandra Dallas*

233

Manitou Springs. The addition of roof overhangs made the international style more liveable in Colorado. *Kendal Atchison*

Denver. If most "modern" houses were a love affair with contemporary materials, this one was an infatuation with cement. This five-level, all-cement house even has cement cupboards. The house originally was painted bright pink. *Sandra Dallas*

Boulder. This house was the latest in contemporary styling inside and out. Its all-electric kitchen with one of the first dishwashers in the state won a $1,000 award in 1939 from a national electric association. *Kendal Atchison*

Denver. The best contemporary kitchens boasted electrical appliances, built-in cupboards, and yards of sleek countertops. More modest kitchens could also be modernized, such as this one with its stainless steel counters and marbleized doors on the gas stove. *Courtesy Denver Public Library Western History Department.*

Pueblo. Even Christmas decorations cannot disguise the severe lines of this international-style house. *Courtesy Pueblo Library District.*

Epilogue

T HE PENT-UP DEMAND for housing that followed World War II caused a building explosion in Colorado. Not only were native sons eager to return to hearth and home in Colorado, but GIs from all over the country who had been stationed in the state during the war came back to set up permanent housekeeping.

Many of these postwar homeowners returned to the comfortable houses on tree-lined city streets they had known as children, but the majority opted for that enticing new life-style they found in a place called suburbia. The result was a population explosion accompanied by a housing boom.

Developers were happy to oblige these new home buyers, and all across Colorado street after street of cookie-cutter houses were thrown up at breakneck speed on the prairies surrounding Colo-

Denver. Once a curiosity that attracted Sunday drivers, this postwar house was an oddity because of its butterfly roof. Denverites were not familiar with internal drains. *Sandra Dallas*

239

Eads. Coloradans never quite got over their penchant for living in castles.
Sandra Dallas

Vail. Alpine architecture became popular in Colorado ski areas. *Kendal Atchison*

Vail. Some of the best contemporary domestic architecture is not in the cities but in the high-living ski communities. *Kendal Atchison*

rado's largest cities. There were ranch-style homes with everything on one floor, split-level houses with their clusters of stairs, and modern houses with cinder-block fireplaces and butterfly roofs. They all had carports and patios with barbecue grills, and they were neatly set apart from each other by mile upon mile of chain-link fence. The houses were identical to those being built in Cleveland and Los Angeles and Detroit. If they were unimaginative and pedestrian, however, these houses also were inexpensive, available with no-down-payment Veterans Administration loans, and they allowed thousands of young families to become homeowners.

As they became more affluent and their families larger, this postwar generation demanded larger homes, fancier decors, and more convenience. A more affluent suburbia was built to meet their needs. There were washer-dryer combinations and all-electric kitchens; garages replaced carports, as station wagons replaced Nash Ramblers and Studebakers. At the same time, Coloradans,

Basalt. Another postwar housing phenomenon was a preoccupation with shapes. *Kendal Atchison*

South of **Alamosa.** The geodesic dome, which offered an intriguing if unconventional use of space, became popular in the 1960s and 1970s, particularly in Colorado communes. *Sandra Dallas*

243

Breckenridge. The ubiquitous A-frame was the most common postwar shape, especially in ski areas where its relatively inexpensive construction made it popular for use as a second home. *Sandra Dallas*

Blanca. Another postwar phenomenon was the trailer house. Originally designed for vacationers, manufactured housing (a.k.a. mobile homes, a.k.a. trailers) eventually became a permanent part of the Colorado landscape. *Sandra Dallas*

Genesee. Dubbed the "clamshell house" and the "flying saucer house," this 1966 house was used as a setting in the futuristic Woody Allen movie *Sleeper.* Architect Charles Deaton designed it as a "sculptural architecture." *Courtesy Charles Deaton.*

who had always shied away from multiunit dwellings as smacking faintly of living above the store, embraced new housing concepts such as condominiums and townhouses. Regardless of what they were called, they still looked like Cleveland, which was not surprising, since national builders began to dominate the housing industry.

As time passed, homeowners demanded a combination of modern convenience and an aura of the past, and builders responded with a bag of nostalgic tricks. Phony Tudors and phony Georgians were built. There was a pseudo–Mediterranean style and later a pseudo–tropical deco. In the mountains, turrets and gingerbread trim were pasted onto conventional houses to form nouveau Victorians.

Despite this mass production, Colorado continued to turn out a few unusual houses, many of them in vacation areas. The A-frame, for example, which was inexpensive to build, became a ubiquitous shape in Colorado ski areas. Geodesic domes were favored by hippie communes. Lavish Austrian or Alpine-style houses met the need for second homes in expensive mountain towns. On oc-

245

casion, imaginative architects turned out intriguing one-of-a-kind new shapes and styles, generally for well-heeled clients.

For the most part, however, Colorado's wealthy who wanted new homes settled for simply bigger and more expensive. They demanded huge building lots in costly enclaves, often in semirural communities that were walled off against the curious. Independent oilman and movie mogul Marvin Davis, for example, posts guards around his 16,000-square-foot, ten-bath house in Englewood.

Many of these *faux* castles are little more than overgrown suburban tract houses. "It is hard to design a house that looks well and is that big," noted the mayor of one impacted town. Indeed, Cherry Hills Village, adjacent to Denver, was so concerned about the nouveau estates with their outsize homes that it called for a limit on house size.

To those of us who believe that imaginative housing design stopped for the most part with the onset of World War II, these paeans to bad taste and mass production represent the nadir in Colorado housing. But we may be wrong. After all, contemporaries of the empire builders found their instant and ostentatious stone castles an affront to good taste, and for years Americans viewed Victorian architecture as overblown and silly. Even the sensible bungalows and Denver squares were remodeled by subsequent generations who added bay windows and porchless stoops to hide the old-fashioned lines.

Every housing style has its day—and its off day. Another generation may view nostalgically the multiple levels and family rooms and patios of postwar housing. What is tasteless today could become desirably quaint tomorrow. Future Coloradans may look at today's A-frames and tract houses as one more chapter in the rich story of Colorado's historic homes.

246

Bibliography

Books

Abele, Deborah Edge. *The Westside: An Introduction to Its History and Architecture.* Colorado Springs: City of Colorado Springs, 1983.

Adams, Eugene H., Dorsett, Lyle W., and Pulcipher, Robert S. *The Pioneer Western Bank—First of Denver: 1860–1980.* Denver: First Interstate Bank of Denver, 1984.

Arps, Louisa Ward. *Denver in Slices.* Denver: Sage Books, 1959.

Backus, Harriet Fish. *Tomboy Bride.* Boulder: Pruett Publishing Co., 1969.

Bancroft, Caroline. *Tabor's Matchless Mine and Lusty Leadville.* Boulder: Johnson Publishing Co., 1967.

———. *The Melodrama of Wolhurst.* Denver: Golden Press, 1952.

Barker, Jane Valentine. *Historic Homes of Boulder County.* Boulder: Pruett Publishing Co., 1979.

———. *Seventy-Six Historic Homes of Boulder Colorado.* Boulder: Pruett Publishing Co., 1976.

Barns, Cass G. *The Sod House.* Lincoln: University of Nebraska Press, 1970.

Batschelet, Ralph J. *The Flick and I.* Smithtown: Exposition Press, 1981.

Brettell, Richard R. *Historic Denver: The Architects and the Architecture 1858–1893.* Denver: Historic Denver, Inc., 1973.

Crofutt, George A. *Crofutt's Grip-Sack Guide of Colorado 1885.* Boulder: Johnson Books, 1966.

Davis, Sally, and Baldwin, Betty. *Denver Dwellings and Descendants.* Denver: Sage Books, 1963.

Downing, Andrew Jackson. *Victorian Cottage Residences.* New York: Dover Publications, Inc., 1981.

Ellis, Anne. *The Life of An Ordinary Woman.* Lincoln, University of Nebraska Press, 1980.

Etter, Don D. *Auraria: Where Denver Began.* Boulder: Colorado Associated University Press, 1972.

———. *Denver Going Modern.* Denver: Graphic Impressions, Inc., 1977.

Ferril, Thomas Hornsby. *New and Selected Poems.* Westport: Greenwood Press, 1970.

———. *Westering.* New Haven: Yale University Press. 1935.

Foley, Mary Mix. *The American House.* New York: Harper & Row, 1980.

Foote, Mary Hallock. *A Victorian Gentlewoman in the Far West.* San Marino: Huntington Library, 1980.

Fossett, Frank. *Colorado: Its Gold and Silver Mines, Ranches, and Pleasure Resorts.* Glorieta: Rio Grande Press, Inc., 1976.

Fowler, Gene. *Timber Line.* New York City: Blue Ribbon Books, Inc., 1935.

Fowler, Orson S. *The Octagon House: A Home for All.* New York: Dover Publications, Inc., 1973.

Freed, Elaine, and Barber, David. *Historic Sites and Structures, El Paso County, Colorado.* Colorado Springs: El Paso County Land Use Development, ca. 1977.

Frost, Hunter S. *Art, Artifacts, Architecture: Fountain Valley School.* Colorado Springs: Tiverton Press, 1980.

Gehlert, Vera. *Longmont Architectural Heritage.* Denver: (n.p.) 1976.

Griswold, Don, and Griswold, Jean. *Colorado's Century of "Cities".* Denver: Smith-Brooks Printing Co., 1958.

Hafen, LeRoy R., and Hafen, Ann W. *Reports from Colorado: The Wildman Letters 1859–1865.* Glendale: Arthur H. Clark Co., 1961.

Hall, Frank. *History of the State of Colorado.* 4 vols. Chicago: Blakely Printing Co., 1889, 1890, 1891, 1895.

Hill, Alice Polk. *Tales of the Colorado Pioneers.* Glorieta: Rio Grande Press, Inc., 1976.

Hopton, Heather, and Shuldener, Lilo. *Aspen's Early Days: A Walking Tour.* Boulder: Johnson Publishing Co., 1978.

Ingersoll, Ernest. *Crest of the Continent.* Chicago: R. R. Donnelley & Sons Co., ca. 1885.

Ingle, Marjorie I. *Mayan Revival Style.* Salt Lake City: Peregrine Smith Books, 1984.

Johnson, Cathryne, ed. *Bent's Old Fort.* Denver: Colorado Historical Society, 1977.

Kerouac, Jack. *On the Road.* New York: Viking, 1957.

Kohl, Edith Eudora. *Denver's Historic Mansions.* Denver: Sage Books, 1957.

Lavender, David. *Bent's Fort.* Garden City: Doubleday & Co., 1954.

McAlester, Virginia, and McAlester, Lee. *A Field Guide to American Houses.* New York: Alfred A. Knopf, 1984.

McCrystal Design and Long Hoeft Architects. *Curtis Park: A Case Study for Neighborhood Revitalization Utilizing Historic Preservation.* Denver: Historic Denver, Inc., 1982.

McFarlane, Ida Kruse, and Van Riper, Melicent, editors. *The Glory That Was Gold.* Central City: Central City Opera House Association, 1940.

McLean, Evalyn Walsh. *Father Struck It Rich.* Boston: Little, Brown & Co., 1936.

Morris, Langdon. *Denver Landmarks*. Denver: Charles W. Cleworth, 1979.

Neeley, Cynthia Wadsworth. *Georgetown Landmarks*. Georgetown: Georgetown Society, Inc., 1978.

Noel, Thomas Jacob. *Richthofen's Montclair*. Denver: Graphic Impressions, Inc., 1976.

Pearce, Sarah J. *A Guide to Colorado Architecture*. Denver: State Historical Society of Colorado, 1983.

Pearring, John, and Pearring, Joanne. *The Walking Tour: An Historical Guide to Manitou Springs*. Manitou Springs: Manitou Springs Development Co., 1983.

Poppeliers, John, Chambers, S. Allen, and Schwartz, Nancy B. *What Style Is It?* Washington: The Preservation Press, 1981.

Propst, Nell Brown. *Forgotten People: A History of the South Platte Trail*. Boulder: Pruett Publishing Co., 1979.

Richardson, Albert D. *Beyond the Mississippi*. Hartford: American Publishing Co., 1869.

Rifkind, Carole. *A Field Guide to American Architecture*. New York: New American Library, 1980.

Scamehorn, Lee. *A. E. Humphreys and Sons*. Denver: Colorado Historical Society, 1984.

Seiden, O. J. *Denver's Richthofen Castle*. Denver: Stonehenge Books, 1980.

Smiley, Jerome C. *History of Denver*. Evansville: Unigraphic, Inc., 1971.

Smith, Jean Walton, and Walsh, Elaine Colvin. *Queen of the Hill*. Denver: Colorado Historical Society, 1979.

Smith, Marian (Poppy). *Healy House and Dexter Cabin*. Denver: State Historical Society of Colorado, 1962.

Sprague, Marshall. *Money Mountain*. Boston: Little, Brown & Co., 1953.

————. *Newport in the Rockies*. Chicago: Sage Books, 1980.

Stickley, Gustav. *Craftsman Homes*. New York, Dover Publications, Inc., 1979.

Stone, Wilbur Fisk. *History of Colorado*. 3 vols. Chicago: S. J. Clarke Publishing Co., 1918.

Street, Julian. *Abroad At Home*. Garden City: Garden City Publishing Co., 1926.

Taylor, Morris F. *Trinidad, A Centennial Town*. Trinidad: O'Brien Printing & Stationery Co., 1976.

Vickers, W. B. *History of the City of Denver, Arapahoe County, and Colorado*. Chicago: O. L. Baskin & Co., 1880.

Welsch, Roger L. *Sod Walls*. Broken Bow, Neb.: Purcells, Inc., 1968.

West, William Allen, and Etter, Don D. *Curtis Park: A Denver Neighborhood*. Boulder: Colorado Associated University Press, 1980.

Whitacre, Christine. *Molly Brown: Denver's Unsinkable Lady*. Denver: Historic Denver, Inc., 1984.

Wiberg, Ruth Eloise. *Rediscovering Northwest Denver: Its History, Its People, Its Landmarks.* Boulder: Pruett Publishing Co., 1976.

Wilcox, Rhoda Davis. *The Bells of Manitou.* Colorado Springs: Little London Press, 1973.

Willison, George F. *Here They Dug the Gold.* New York: Reynal & Hitchcock, 1946.

Wolle, Muriel Sibell. *Stampede to Timberline.* Denver: Sage Books, 1962.

Articles

Margolis, Eric. "Colorado's Coal People." *Colorado Heritage* 4 (1984): 10–24.

Markoff, Dena S. "The Sugar Industry in the Arkansas River Valley: National Beet Sugar Company." *The Colorado Magazine* (Winter, 1978): 69–92.

Wolle, Muriel S. "Early Mining Camp Architecture." *1953 Brand Book* 9:185–204. Denver: Denver Westerners, 1954.

Brochures

Anonymous. *A Visit to Victorian Highlands.* Denver: Historic Denver, Inc. (n.d.)

———. *Baca House, Bloom House, Pioneer Museum.* Denver: Colorado Historical Society (n.d.)

———. *Bowman-White House.* Georgetown: Georgetown Society, Inc. (n.d.)

———. *Cooks Tour.* Denver: Smith College, 1967.

———. *The DeLuxe Guide in Living Color to the Incomparable Grand Trianon Art Museum.* Colorado Springs: John W. Metzger, 1964.

———. *Fort Garland.* Denver: Colorado Historical Society (n.d.).

———. *The Grant-Humphreys Mansion.* Denver: Colorado Historical Society (n.d.)

———. *Heyday on Quality Hill.* Denver: Historic Denver, Inc. (n.d.)

———. *The Historic Denver House Tour: Belcaro Area.* Denver: Historic Denver, Inc., 1978.

———. *Historic Denver House Tour 1975.* Denver: Historic Denver, Inc., 1975.

———. *Historic Denver House Tour 1976.* Denver: Historic Denver, Inc., 1976.

———. *Historic Denver's Curtis Park House and Neighborhood Tour.* Denver: Historic Denver, Inc., 1980.

———. *Historic Walking Tours of Aspen.* Aspen: Aspen Historical Society (n.d.)

———. *History of the Rudd Cabin and Stone Home* (n.p.) (n.d.)

————. *Humboldt Island*. Denver: Historic Denver, Inc., 1982.

————. *Humboldt Street House Tour*. Denver: Historic Denver, Inc., 1974.

————. *The Plains Conservation Center for Colorado*. (n.p.) (n.d.)

Underhill Lonnie E. *John A. Thatcher*. Pueblo: Pueblo Metropolitan Museum Association, 1980.

————. *Margaret A. Thatcher*. Pueblo: Pueblo Metropolitan Museum Association, 1980.

————. *Rosemount Mansion*. Pueblo: Pueblo Metropolitan Museum Association, 1980.

U.S. Department of the Interior, National Park Service. *Bent's Old Fort*. (No location) (n.d.)

Government Documents

Nominations for the National Register of Historic Places, U.S. Department of the Interior, National Park Service.

Newspapers

Colorado Heritage News (Denver)
Colorado Prospector (Denver)
Denver Post
Denver Times
Historic Denver News
Pueblo Chieftain
Pueblo Star-Journal
Rocky Mountain News (Denver)
The Daily News (Denver)
The Western Architect and Building News (Denver)

Index

Colorado Homes,
designed by Frank O. Williams, was set in various sizes of Bembo by
G&S Typesetters, Inc., and printed offset on 70-pound Warren's Flokote
by McNaughton & Gunn, Inc., with case binding by John H. Dekker &
Sons.